Blood Bond

Alex Tyson

Copyright © 2017 by Alex Tyson
ISBN: 0692976272
ISBN 13: 9780692976272

Dedication

I would like to acknowledge my mother Clementine Tyson-Salters for her endless prayers and reinforcing that God can and will make all things possible.

Part One

CHAPTER 1

What's Going On?

Darlington, South Carolina; July 1972

CAROL WAS USED to hiding in the closet for a long time whenever she was the hider, but she started to feel as if she'd been in there forever! To pass time, she'd counted backwards from one hundred. Barely whispering, she had recited her father's favorite bedtime story about growing up in Tupelo, Mississippi and fishing with his father on the banks of the Mississippi River. By the end of the story, she hadn't even heard a door hinge squeak or a floor-board creak. Maybe Daddy had stopped being the seeker and had turned into a hider, she'd thought.

"Daddy, Daddy, come out, come out, wherever you are," she sing-sang softly.

As she padded down the avocado enamel painted hallway, the sound of her father's Marvin Gaye record blaring from the hi-fi stereo in the living room got a little louder. Marvin was singing, "And all He asks of us, oh yeah, is we give each other love." Carol know the song well; it was the front side on one of her father's favorite 45s. She hummed along as she passed the doorway.

"I know where you are," Carol called out. "Betcha I can find you!"

She checked the hall closet first. It was his all-time favorite hiding place, back behind the coats, where he'd lurk until she opened the door. He would jump out and yell, "Boo!" and she would run, screaming gleefully, and he would chase her and tickle her, then hug her and kiss her on the head and say, "I love you, sweet pea." Well, at least, when she was younger, that's how it always went. It was hard to get Daddy to play hide and seek anymore. After two weeks of daily pleading, he'd finally given in.

3

She crept toward the closet stealthily, trying to surprise him. She flung open the closet door. "Gotcha!" she shouted as loudly as she could. But there was no response. To her dismay, no Daddy.

Carol leaned over and looked under the coats. No legs. She probed the coats with her hand and felt them shimmy back and forth on their hangers. No Daddy.

Almost immediately, she perked up. No, he wasn't going to fool her this time, she decided. She skipped down the stairs to the basement. The last time they'd played this game, her father had hidden in the cellar behind the furnace.

"Dad-dy," she called playfully. Then, a little louder. "Daaad-dy."

To her surprise, he wasn't in any of the basement corners. Bewildered, she climbed back up the stairs.

"Daddy!" she called louder than before as she reached the top landing. She was running out of places to look. Slowly, she paced toward her parents' bedroom near the back of the two-bedroom duplex. With each step she took, her sandals squeaked on the hardwood floor. Was it the bass drum she still felt vibrating through the floor, or was that her heartbeat?

"Daddy, I don't want to play hide-and go-seek anymore," she murmured. The door creaked a little, revealing the neatly furnished bedroom with the chenille bedspread and small faux wood dresser. Still no sign of her father.

Marvin was singing a different song now, "What's Going On?" "Mother, mother, there's too many of you crying; brother, brother, brother, there's far too many of you dying..." It was her heartbeat, she realized, looking down at the pulsing spot on her chest beneath the lightweight summer dress.

Suddenly she noticed that eerily familiar smell, kind of like burning pinecones, coming from the living room. Usually her father forbade her to go into the front room, but this time she didn't care. As she approached the room, there was a repeated muffle, crackling, and then the needle skipped.

"War is not the answer, for—" *pop! Skick!* "War is not the answer, for—" *pop! Skick!* began to play over and over as the needle jumped back again and again.

Her eyes opened wide, Carol froze midstride. Her father, head thrown back, eyes rolled back in his skull, sat slumped in his aged arm chair."

Carol dashed to his side. "Daddy, what's the matter? Wake up!" she cried, shaking her father's shoulder, but he slumped over, his head bouncing off his knee.

She knew that sometimes her father acted strangely since coming home from Vietnam. "Soldier's disease," her mother called it. This was exactly what Carol's mother, Josephine, had told Miss Penny next door. Miss Penny was Josephine's longtime best friend, and Miss Penny's daughter Kim was Carol's best friend too. She remembered her mother and Miss Penny sitting on the porch one night, after the girls had been sent to bed. The rusty springs on the porch swing creaked and the crickets chirped together and Josephine had said, "I heard the soldiers came back depressed, but he's nothing like he used to be. Nothing at all." Carol didn't know what her mother meant, but she knew it was the saddest thing her mother had ever said.

"Daddy, talk to me," Carol cried, tears dripping onto her cheeks.

With all the strength she could muster, Carol lifted her father's head from his knees. In a cupping swoop, she hit her father on his face, trying to rouse him. Almost instantly, he fell backwards, his head dangling on the flowered armchair. That's when she saw the needle still stuck in his arm. Stunned and speechless, Carol hit him on his forearm. His arm felt limp. It was still warm.

"War is not the answer, for—" *pop! Skick!* "War is not the answer, for—" *pop! Skick!*

After five more small slaps couldn't wake him, Carol stumbled to the front porch to wait for her mother. She wanted to go next door to Miss Penny's, but in her head she could hear her mother's voice: "What happens in this house stays in this house." So she waited.

Sunset gold slipped into amber clouds, and then everything was one giant silhouette. "Mom should be home any time now," she thought as she rocked back and forth on the porch swing. Would it really be telling their private family business if she went to Miss Penny's house?

Maybe her father was just asleep. Over the summer when she was out of school, Daddy would babysit her while her mother caught two buses and went to work at Fuller's Market across town. Carol remembered when Daddy used to work, but that was before the war. She vaguely remembered how he used to tickle her before, too. He used to be a fun daddy; a happy daddy... those were her favorite memories of him, that big smile, that laugh that could fill a room with so much love that nothing bad could get in.

A couple of weeks ago, Carol had found him curled up asleep on the tea-colored shag carpeted floor between the dresser and the bed in her parents' room. She thought it was odd—he'd never done that before—but when he woke up, he seemed fine. Sometimes she liked how her daddy was since he came from the war, because he'd play with her as if he was any other child her age. Sometimes, though, he would do something that scared her, like that time he rolled up like a kitten on the floor. She was never afraid of him, but sometimes Carol wondered if he could really hear her.

Carol sat and picked at a scab on her right knee as gray settled over the silhouette of the neighborhood. Then, in the distance, Carol spotted her mom trudging down the street, carrying a bag of groceries. The number 22 bus had just dropped her off at the corner. Work must have kept her late again.

As fast as her eight-year-old legs would carry her, Carol ran down the street to meet her mother.

Carol felt relief flood down to her feet as she reached her Mom. She felt everything would be okay. Mom can fix it, she thought, grabbing her mother's skirt and trotting alongside her. Her mother's face was a stoic African mask.

"Mom," she called out, when she was a little closer. "Something's wrong with Daddy."

"Where's Mitchell?" her mother demanded. This had happened before. She only called Daddy "Mitchell" when she was frustrated with him. "He's supposed to be babysitting you."

"Daddy's in the living room, and he won't wake up," Carol panted, as she tried to catch her breath while skipping along, two steps to each of her mother's giant strides. She took a deep gulp. "His eyes are open but he won't move. I

6

didn't know what to do, Mommy. I've been sitting on the porch waiting for you forever."

Josephine's pace picked up immediately. "It'll be all right, child. He's prob'ly just fine." Carol skip-ran alongside her mother, looking up at the mask for clues.

As they reached the porch stairs, Josephine stopped and turned to Carol. "Go next door to Ms. Penny's house and stay with her children until I call you. Tell Ms. Penny to come over."

"No, Mommy, please—I want to go with you."

Josephine's eyes told the tale: end of discussion. She'd said it so often while giving Carol that look that Carol didn't even need to hear the words anymore. The decision was final.

"War is not the answer, for—" *pop! Skick!* "War is not the answer, for—" *pop! Skick!*

A creak, and Josephine opened the front door. "Mitchell!"

She stepped into the entrance hallway and the darkness seemed to push into the house and fill up all the space. She took seven slow steps toward the living room off the front hallway.

"Mitch," she said, softly, kind of like she used to whisper into his ear at night, but this time she was praying out of fear. He'd fallen asleep while listing to his music, like usual, right? That's exactly what had happened the week before: she had approached him, at first, and seen his eyes were open, and then he'd blinked and smiled faintly and said, "I'm just noddin'…" She'd put her arm around him and they'd walked to the bedroom together.

His eyes were wide open again. A seizure, perhaps?—it was a possible side effect—but no, the air smelled burnt. Then her eyes followed his arm down from the shoulder, and she saw the rubber band and the protruding needle.

Josephine cupped her mouth to hold back the scream welling up in her chest. The scream was sucking energy out of her legs, and an flash of dizziness passed over her.

She sat on the armchair and concentrated on slowing her breathing. She had to remain calm for Carol's sake. Suddenly, hearing a knock at the door, she turned.

"Josephine! What's wrong?" Miss Penny walked in without waiting for a response. She rushed into the living room, and saw the young wife cradling her husband's head in her arm. "He's getting cold," Josephine said hoarsely.

Miss Penny took one look, then pivoted around and rushed to the phone and called 911. Josephine called her mother, and then Mitch's mom.

"War is not the answer, for—" *pop! Skick!* "War is not the answer, for—" *pop! Skick!*

Josephine had known many things about Mitchell, but she'd had no idea that he used drugs.

CHAPTER 2

Funeral, Saturday morning, 11:00 a.m.

One Week Later

THE FAMILY TRAILED into First Baptist Ebenezer Church, following the funeral director. Josephine, back ramrod straight, head held high, wore a black suit, long gloves, and a veiled hat. Meanwhile, Carol's steps fell unevenly as she followed her mother. Tear streaks painted pinstripes on her face. "Mommy, my chest hurts." She pointed to her heart. Her mother patted her shoulder wordlessly as they took a seat in the front pew with the family.

At Josephine's request, the casket was closed. She would not give the town busybodies any satisfaction. Instead, she had Mitchell's enlistment portrait, an eight-by-ten picture of him in dress uniform standing in front of the flag, posted on top of the bronze casket. Aromas of chrysanthemums, lilies, and roses wafted from the sanctuary.

"Why, Lord?" Mitch's mother, Miss Lucy, cried over and over in between heaves and sobs. Her husband, Mitchell Senior, stroked her back.

"Mommy, when is Daddy coming back?"

Josephine squeezed her daughter's hand but didn't avert her eyes from the casket. Then she let go of Carol's hand and folded the memorial service program in half vertically, and Mitch's 20-year-old face narrowed and disappeared into the crease. She pushed the folded program into her purse.

The First Baptist Ebenezer Church Choir had been waiting on the risers. The choir director, Alvin Brown, a fiery-spirited, stocky man in his late sixties, mounted the podium and gave a silent measure with his timing hand.

The singers broke into "Coming Home To Heaven," which they followed with "Amazing Grace."

Carol reviewed the funeral program: Organ Prelude, "Precious Lord;" Processional, "It Is Well With My Soul;" Scriptures, of which there were several; and at last, Eulogy, Rev. N. Austin.

Minister Nathaniel Austin paused for a moment at the lectern and removed his reading glasses.

"Here we are again to bury another young man; a defender of our country; a father; a child of God. He goes to the grave too early—forgive me, Lord, for questioning your will, but it feels like it's all too soon! His mother and father, Lucille and Mitchell Bolden, Senior, sit in the front pew with his wife, Josephine, and their young daughter, Carol. I've seen it so many times already, with other good young men and their teary-eyed families... and I'm sick of watching it happen."

He descended into the main aisle and slowly paced, looking at each of the gathered faithful.

"This story has been told too many times. This story has to be rewritten for our young Black men. This young man served his country and was given an honorable discharge. But here his body lies today, at the age of twenty-six. Something is wrong with this picture, and I'm going to tell you what: racism, White Supremacy, and this ungodly Vietnam War. This is where we need to place the blame."

"Speak on it," Deacon Harold intoned.

"Mitchell came to Christ at an early age. Of that we can be grateful. Our prayers are with the family and friends in their hour of need. Lord give them strength." An "amen" rippled through the pews.

"Mitch's only daughter, Carol, is eight years old—just a baby. Josephine, a devoted wife and mother, is left to raise their baby girl alone."

"Now, I've heard some of the rumors being whispered about Mitch, but I've known Mitchell since he was a little boy. He matured to be a good man, who loved the Lord Christ."

"Amen!" someone shouted from the back of the church.

"First, you must walk in another man's shoes before you begin to judge. Let's leave the judging to our Father, almighty God." Minister wiped his sweaty brow with a wide white handkerchief.

"Mitch, like many young men, answered the call of duty. He naively but optimistically believed Uncle Sam. He believed that the country needed him to fight for freedom and justice in Vietnam. And that is the main reason he's fallen asleep with the saints on this sad day."

"Where is the freedom and justice in this country for us, for people of color? Why must we still eat the scraps that fall from the master's table? Why is it that in employment, housing, and wealth, we have the lowest collective numbers and the worst collective situation? Once again, we are being used as pawns by this country. What will the government do to us when they no longer need us? Throw us away like Hitler tried to do with the Jews in Nazi Germany?"

"Have mercy!" Brother Williams shouted.

"Black people, we are in a precarious position in this country. Mitchell is not totally responsible for how his life ended. It ended when he was born in a pool of blood as a Black man. Let me explain."

"The black warriors on the front lines in Vietnam have suffered a higher rate of death and dismemberment. Let's not forget the use of Agent Orange and its effect on our veterans. Yet, we have no programs to assist young men coming back from the war with diseases that affect not only their physical and mental health, but the lives of their wives and children. They have to fight for jobs, fair housing, higher education and welfare for the disabled. And at the fronts of those lines, just like the battle lines, are filled with young Black men. We are being used once again by this country. First, our ancestors were brought here in chains. Then they were raped, plundered, beaten, and worked into early graves.

"Then we went through Jim Crow, segregation, and lynching. But now we have a new enemy. It is the epidemic of drugs being poured into the Black community. And this is no accident. No, no, my brothers and sisters, this is not by accident; it is by design!" Scattered light applause and "Mmmhmm"s began as Reverend Austin's voice rasped with conviction. "It's no accident that more drugs and guns are being sold in our community and the death rate of our young people has risen to a level that anywhere else would be universally recognized as alarming; problematic; unsustainable. Top this with police brutality and their illegitimate but condoned killing of our young men."

"So you see the plan, young people. If you don't die defending the system, the system will give you every chance to get hooked on drugs—and I'm not talking about simple reefer, here. I'm talking about heroin, cocaine, and LSD. Young people, wake up! Hear my words! Remember what I'm saying. Don't let Mitch's death be in vain. Don't go down this same road. Who was there to help Mitch? Who could he turn to for help?"

"Surely, not the government, who would arrest him. The army, the very ones who caused the Vietnam nightmare that our young Black men lived in, and then caused drug problems in many of our veterans. Mitch is another victim of the genocide we see happening in our community. This "final solution," this holocaust of the New World, this government-sponsored extermination is by design. It was made by people who see no value in us as humans. Be wise, now, and protect yourself. Don't become another victim.

"O Lord," he said, thrusting his arms open wide, palms toward the ceiling, "receive your son and our dear brother into your loving arms, where all your adopted children sit at the banquet table with you, the author of all colors, the fount of love and blessing. Give us mercy and strength. We ask all this in the name of Jesus Christ our Lord."

The "amen" resounded, and then the silence returned, broken only by the sounds of the pallbearers' shoes clacking on the floor as they bore the casket toward the door.

CHAPTER 3

Repast

Later That Day

CAROL'S BLACK PATENT leather shoes and ruffled socks stuck out in front of her, then billowed out behind her as she swung high in the tree swing her daddy had built for her last summer—his first summer home from Vietnam. Her shoes were so shiny she could see her white cotton underwear reflected in the patent leather toes as she pumped her legs outwards.

Although she appeared to be aimlessly lost in thought, she was listening intently to every word of a conversation nearby. Her mother used to always reprimand Carol for doing that. "Stay out of grown folks' business!" she would chide. But today was different. Her mother seemed distant, far away, as though motionless and sinking in deep water.

Carol stared through the trees, recalling the reminiscent conversations of her parents' close friends. "Inseparable…" She knew they were talking about her parents.

"He was just never the same after he went to 'Nam." Josephine's voice lamented over and over to the different comforting church members who leaned over and hugged her.

After returning from the cemetery, everyone had driven to Josephine's house, where the repast was held in the backyard. The church had provided white fold-up wooden chairs, which were neatly circled. The various thick-waisted women of the Culinary Ministry had provided the food, which included fried chicken, collard greens, macaroni and cheese, potato salad, seven-layer coconut cake, and sweet potato pie. All this was washed down with mixed strawberry and grape Kool Aid ladled into paper cups from a giant crystal punch bowl.

After everyone was served, Josephine sat and talked quietly under a maple tree with Mitch's buddies from the Army.

From Carol's swing in the tree, the voices floated across the air like a bee's hum. She attuned her ears to the voices and honed in on the conversation.

Just like at the wake, her father's friends were remembering the good times. That night, outside the funeral home, they'd drunk Hennessy and performed ritual libation, pouring their drinks out on the ground. "To Mitch, our boy." "May he rest in peace." "He was the man."

Josephine sat in a small circle with Mitch's army friends, Tyrone, Tim, and Greg. They had often talked to Josephine over the phone when they called for Mitch, but she'd never met them in person until the night of the wake. Carol remembered her father's jocular laugh whenever he talked on the phone with his friends. That was the only time he would laugh since coming back Vietnam: when he talked to his war buddies on the phone.

Greg, a double amputee, shifted in his wheelchair. "I still can't believe he's gone. I mean, how can I still be here and he's not? Life don't make much sense, but death is totally outta hand."

Tyrone smoothed over his full ebony beard, then looked with piercing phosphorous eyes at the group as he spoke. "Mitch was good people. We always said we were going to have a reunion, meet the wives, catch up on the happenings, you know. But I never thought this would be the occasion." He shook his head ruefully.

"It's ironic." Josephine wrung her hands. "I waited faithfully for my husband to come home. Taking care of our daughter and working part-time kept me busy. Mitchell often wrote to say he couldn't wait to return to me and Carol, and that as soon as he returned, he would enroll in accounting classes and finish college."

Tim chimed in. "When I first met Mitch, all he talked about was you, his kid, finishing school, and taking care of his family. You know, he wanted to use the GI Bill to buy your family a home."

Tyrone exhaled with frustration. "This GI Bill seems to only work for the white boys. They don't seem to have a problem getting a mortgage approved. I ran into White Tommy from our unit and he said he got a loan and he and his family are already living in their colonial."

"Yeah," Greg piped up. "Mitch told me he was turned down for a loan because he was only receiving disability. And you weren't making that much at the grocery store."

Josephine's voice sounded surprised. "I didn't know he wanted to get us a home. He was so withdrawn when he came from the army. I could hardly get him to talk! The most he would do is babysit Carol and sometimes he would play with her like in the old times." She looked off dreamily as if she could still see Mitch.

"He said his mind was too messed up to go to work yet," Tyrone explained. "He couldn't get over all the killings and bombings he saw in Vietnam. He wanted to get a job, though."

Josephine nodded. "I know they discharged him early because of his injury. I didn't know when he'd be able to work again."

"Tyrone, you was with him when he had the accident, weren't you, man?" Tim asked.

"Yeah, that I was," Tyrone replied. "He sprained his ankle and we had miles to walk. The medics gave him morphine to kill the pain."

Tim glanced at the grieving group. "I never thought he'd get hooked on drugs. When he came to the service, he didn't even drink a beer. He didn't smoke. We used to tease him about how he was so square. He never got wasted with us."

"So, he finally comes home. Now this." Josephine shook her head and began to cry softly. Then she shook her head and struggled to regain her composure. "If only he'd told me. I would have worked with him. I would have gotten him some help."

Josephine continued, as if she was speaking directly to her dead husband. "We never had secrets from each other." Her bottom lip quivered. "Or at least I never did. How could you lie to me, Mitch? You never told me you had a drug problem."

Greg tried to comfort Josephine. "I lost my legs over there, but that wasn't all I lost. It's hard to come back to the world. They use up our youth, then throw us away like garbage. Don't be so hard on him, Josephine."

Suddenly, Carol's grandmother, Lucy, called her to help put the food away. Carol leaped out of the swing and ran toward the house. She wanted to be with her mom, but she complied with her grandmother's request.

Carol started to pick up items left near the circle of chairs. For a moment, she cast a glance at her mother. Josephine looked so tired... wrinkles pinched up her face, black bags had formed under her eyes, and her head seemed too heavy for her to hold up easily.

Carol picked up two empty bowls, watching her Mom's eyes turn to slits in her face as she fought back more tears.

"Poor Mitch," Josephine said, "he never adjusted to the disrespect he felt when he returned home from the war."

Tyrone sighed. "Well, when we arrived in San Francisco in our army uniforms wearing our Purple Hearts and badges of honor, this hippie girl came up to Mitch and spit on him. 'Baby killer!' she screamed.

"I'll never forgot how shocked Mitch looked. He thought we'd be coming home to welcoming parades. Oh, it was a parade all right, just not a happy one. The hippies were welcoming the soldiers home with taunts, burning flags, and buckets of red paint. This Vietnam war did our men in—especially Black men."

Carol's hands started to shake so much that she couldn't carry anything. She scurried inside and hid until most of the people had departed. Mitch's mother, Lucy, saw Carol running to her room and began to bid everyone firm farewells.

⊷▆◉ ◉▆⊶

Eventually the memory of the funeral began to fade, but there was still plenty of hardship to go around. Even with the little check Josephine got from VA as a surviving spouse, plus a small stipend for Carol, they still had a hard time making ends meet.

Josephine often worked two jobs. She spent a little bit of time with Carol on her days off. On those days, she was physically present, but mentally missing in action. Being the single parent exhausted her, and eventually she stopped trying to seem excited and engaged. She simply slept whenever she could. For the next several years, Carol learned and practiced the art, the gift, and the curse of solitude.

⭈⬛ ⬛⭇

Sometimes Carol liked to reminisce about how happy her life had been before her father's death. She saw her childhood divided into two parts: one before Mitch's death, and one after.

Before her father went to Vietnam, she could remember how he and her mother often bathed her and got her ready for bed. Mitch and Carol would hold hands with her as they said nighttime prayers. Sometimes, in the middle of the prayers, she would look up to see her parents looking at each other. The way they looked at each other radiated love. It was a mutual moment that seemed to stretch out into forever, far beyond the prayer and on through the night.

Her mom would lay out Carol's church clothes the night before. They'd drive to church together and walk in, the picture of a lovely young family.

The family's weekly routine consisted of church on Sunday. After service, they would go to one of the large traditional Sunday afternoon dinners with Mitch's folks or Josephine's. Monday through Friday, her dad went to work and her mom stayed home to care for her. Saturday was house cleaning day. Afterward, Carol and her parents would walk to Ann's Sweet Shop on Main Street. They would get their favorites almost every week: her dad would get a peach sucker, her mom would get a quarter's worth of candy corn and nibble them where the colors changed, and she would grab the biggest fistful of M&M's or Good-n-Plenty that she could manage. They'd walk through the old town and talk to everyone they met, even if it meant they went to bed later than usual.

⭈⬛ ⬛⭇

All this changed when her dad went to Vietnam. After the draft, Mitch didn't come home for a long time. He always used to come through the front door when the puppet show would come on television. But as every day brought another puppet show but not her father, Carol became sadder. Eventually, she stopped watching the puppet show. Still, her dad did not return.

Josephine, who used to be home with Carol every day as a stay-at-home mother, went to work during the day. Carol would spend the days next door at Miss Penny's. Since Miss Penny's daughter, Kim, was Carol's age, they would play all day until Josephine returned.

One of Carol's first memories at Miss Penny's house was a surprise birthday. It had happened on her third birthday. She kept a Polaroid picture of herself blowing out the three tiny candles on a giant cake while Kim and Miss Penny clapped and cheered. That day, Kim had given Carol a big box of crayons and a coloring book that they both ended up sharing. Miss Penny and her husband had given Carol a pretty green cotton dress with matching ruffle panties and socks.

Just as Carol had finished opening the gift, the doorbell rang. "I bet that's your Mom," Mrs. Penny had said.

Josephine had come in, carrying a large present under her arm. "Hi, baby girl," she'd said warmly.

Carol had stretched her chubby baby arms up. "Mommy, I missed you." Josephine had put down the present and smothered Carol's face in kisses.

"Mommy has a surprise for you, baby girl."

Carol always smiled and saw the whole scene in her mind whenever she saw the Polaroid. She kept it on her bedside table. Over the years, the picture started to blur bit by bit, and the colors faded, and the edges greyed, and eventually Carol hid the picture in her Bible on the page where the fifty-first chapter of Isaiah began. And she would read that chapter, long after she could no longer distinguish the faces in the picture. Long after the little slip of photo paper had gone to white, it remained her bookmark, splotched by the occasional tear that not even Carol, alone in her room, could prevent.

Chapter 4

University of Connecticut

Storrs, Connecticut; Fall 1982

KEITH NOTICED CAROL when she walked into College Composition two minutes after ten o'clock. She was rushing, as if she were still trying to be on time. The classroom was already filled with students and she scanned the room, trying to find a seat before the professor started to speak.

Keith pointed to an empty seat next to him. She gracefully moved across the room, navigating the aisles of the giant lecture hall and moving around other students and their book bags. She was wearing dark blue jeans with a red jacket and a white embroidered blouse.

"You must be a dancer," he commented as she sat down, sighed, and brushed her bangs out of her eyes.

"How did you know that?" Carol lifted an eyebrow.

"The way your body moves," he said. "I'm not trying to be fresh or disrespectful, but I think you're beautiful. You look like a ballet dancer."

He cleared his throat. "I'm Keith Davidson." He extended his hand to shake Carol's.

She hesitated. Finally, she took his hand and smiled. "Are you one of those charming Southern boys I was warned about?" she asked with a gently lilting tease.

"No; I assure you, I'm a gentleman."

"I'm Carol."

Keith flashed his smile and she loved it. His pearly white, evenly sized teeth made a sharp contrast to his smooth, dark henna skin.

"Where do you live?" Before she could answer the room went quiet.

The professor, a middle-aged White man with a salt-and-peppered goatee, entered the room, marched straight to the podium, and scanned the room. "I'm Dr. Adams," he said loudly but unenthusiastically. On the nearest blackboard, he wrote his name, "Dr. Paul Adams," as he introduced himself. He passed the syllabus to the front row. "Please pass the syllabus around to the person to your right." He then took attendance, calling role of one hundred twenty six freshmen from the UConn Class of 1986.

After class, Carol and Keith strolled to the student bookstore together to find the required reading material. They talked all the way. Although there was no silent time between them, Keith observed that Carol was more reserved. He found it alluring.

"Where do you live?" Keith asked, taking Carol's books out of her arms.

"I'm in the women's dorm on campus. How about you?"

"The men's dorm in the blue building. What other classes do you have?"

Keith watched her as she pulled out her schedule: history, government, art, and of course, English. Heads bowed, they compared classes.

"This is great! Three of our classes are together! Let's study after the last class this evening, if you don't have other plans."

"Sure," she replied.

"Wait—give me your phone number so I can call you."

She couldn't help but smile as she scribbled the number on a corner of notebook paper. As she handed him the page, Keith gently closed his hand over the note, the tips of his fingers touching Carol's as she held onto the slip of paper for an extra second. "I'll call you at five," he said, drawing his hand back slowly. "I'd like that," she replied, turning slowly and heading toward the dorm.

Later that evening, Keith and Carol found a quiet corner in the library to study. In between studying, they talked in whispered tones. Carol asked, "What made you decide to attend UConn?"

"To get out from living under my dad's shadow. He loves us, but he rules with an iron first, and that includes matters of opinion. If Mom hadn't been in my corner, it never would have happened. Dad isn't sure about the whole firefighter dream. Don't get me wrong. I love my Dad. He's a good man, just military, you know; set in his ways and eager to see me follow in his footsteps. I'm the youngest of the boys, so I'm Mom's pet."

"Where are you from?"

"My family's in Atlanta, Georgia" Keith answered. "How about you? Where are you from?"

"I'm an only child, from Darlington, South Carolina."

"How about your dad? What's he like?"

Carol looked away. "He died when I was young."

"I'm sorry to hear that. Here I am complaining about my Dad."

"It's okay. You didn't know."

"When did he pass?"

"He died when I was eight. My mom has since remarried." Carol's lips pulled toward her cheeks and pinched together.

Keith decided to drop the subject. "We'd better get in the books," he said.

They studied for several hours until it was time to part. Keith walked her back to her dorm.

◦—▸▭◦ ◦▭◂—◦

Through the year, Carol and Keith became best friends. They became inseparable; they studied together, went to football and basketball games, and even school dances.

They kept each other company and they kept each other safe. Keith liked that Carol wasn't more interested in dating than in school, and Carol liked that Keith didn't go to parties.

Keith noticed that during school breaks and holidays that Carol would stay at school. She said she did not wish to go home; she would rather stay back to work and study instead. Every time he would ask Carol about it, she would say, "I don't want to talk about it."

Finally, one overcast November day as they watched other students wheeling their suitcases toward taxis, Carol sniffled and tried to pretend she was congested.

"What is it?" Keith asked knowingly.

"I can't talk about it," she said between hiccups. She couldn't continue. Suddenly she broke down into gut-wrenching sobs. Keith put his arms around her and patted her back.

"I don't want to go home again."

Keith nodded and paused to think about it. "Not ever?"

"Never!"

Keith leaned his head onto hers and waited until the sobs subsided.

CHAPTER 5

Keith and Carol

One Year Later

"BABY, WHAT'S WRONG?" Carol looked up from her political science textbook to see Keith's concerned eyes. Still, she remained silent and averted her gaze.

"You never want to talk about home," Keith probed.

Carol heaved a deep sigh. "There's a reason for that."

"What is it?"

"Well, home is not something I really want to remember." The muscles in Carol's face and neck tightened.

"I worry that not talking about it is hurting you more than talking about it ever could."

"Keith, your family is wonderful. I love going home with you at the holidays and school breaks. They treat me like their blood."

Keith smiled; it was true.

Carol's facial muscles relaxed as she recalled eating at the Davidson family table at Easter. A large, rambunctious bunch, going to the dinner table at his house felt like a cattle call. Keith would grab her hand so she wouldn't get edged out by his big brothers. Then he would lead her to a seat beside his, directly to the right of his father's chair at the head of the table. During meals, conversations bounced off each other as people passed plates clockwise. Beneath the scramble for attention and the constant verbal sparring, the Davidsons' hearts beat as one. It became very clear whenever someone shared with the whole group, and then everyone would make room for reactions and discussion about how to handle the situation. Somehow, everyone's needs could be sacred all at once. She explained it as best she could, and Keith nodded and grinned.

"Yeah, that's true."

"I know you have your differences with your Dad, but he is a reasonable man. He will listen to your point of view. He seems honest and fair-minded. Plus, he'll help you with whatever you want to accomplish."

"Yeah, I guess you're right."

Carol thought about it. She hadn't been this happy since her mother and father were together.

Carol rested her head on Keith's shoulder and gazed off at clouds receding into the eastern horizon. "My home is nothing like yours. The home I left is so different. My stepdad, Ralph, made my life a living hell. He—" she coughed and cleared her throat, and then whispered, "He raped me as soon as he married my mom. I turned thirteen that year."

Keith sat still, stunned.

"When I told my mother, it was three years later. Even though I was sixteen then, she didn't believe me." Carol sniffled and Keith reached for a pocket pack of tissues.

"My mom chose him over me. Can you believe that!? Her only daughter. Her own flesh and blood."

Keith pressed a tissue into Carol's hand, but also squeezed her hand reassuringly. "So that's why you stay at school at semester break, huh?"

Then their eyes conversed in soundless tones of concern, then trust, then relief. Carol dabbed her eyes gently, trying not to smear her eyeliner. She inhaled slowly as her confidence rose.

"There's nothing to go home for. Ralph still lives there. I love my Mom, but I refuse to be under the same roof with him. So, I have to love her from a distance."

They watched the sky together as more clouds marched into the future.

"I know you told me your dad died, but could you tell me about him?"

"His name was Mitchell. He died when I was eight."

Her eyes glazed with tears.

"Oh, I'm sorry to hear that. What was your Dad like?"

"I loved my Dad. He and my mom were high school sweethearts. Our family had a different life back then. It was happy. We were a close knit like yours. I remember my dad playing hide and seek with me. He'd read me bedtime stories and sing silly songs with me. He loved to play Marvin Gaye songs. He'd have the hi-fi blasting in the background."

"And my fondest memories were of playing in his garden. He'd let me water some of the plants and he point out which were weeds. He'd let me play in the dirt. Often my friend Kim joined us. We'd make mud pies, and have tea parties."

"What did your father grow?"

"Green beans, greens, carrots, lettuce, and huge tomatoes. He'd wipe a newly ripe tomato on his pants leg and say, 'Take a bite!' and hand me the best-looking tomato right off the vine."

"My mom would fuss. She'd say, 'Don't give that girl vegetables before they're washed off!'"

"I would bite into it anyway. They were the best tomatoes I've ever had. I can still taste them."

"He'd just throw his head back, and laugh. "It's healthier than the vegetables you buy from the store," he'd say, and then he'd eat the rest of it.

"How big was the garden?"

"It covered half the backyard! We lived in a little two-family duplex. My best friend, Kim, lived next door and we were always together. We'd do our homework together, share secrets and play house. As we grew older, sometimes we went to the movies and we'd trade the candy that we brought at Ann's Sweet Shop. That would be our Saturday afternoon treat. That's what we would do after we finished our house chores. We would just walk and talk. Kim is the only one I told about Ralph, other than my Mom—until now.

"My dad went to the Vietnam war when I was two. He didn't return until I was five years old. His ankle was broken in the war; it never healed right. He was always in pain. He couldn't stand on his legs for too long. He said the bad ankle would go numb pretty quick."

She continued. "He wasn't the same. He didn't walk me to Ann's Sweet Shop anymore. He was in too much pain. He had to take pain pills after that to make it through the day. I didn't understand it then, but he got addicted to painkillers. He replanted his garden, but it was never exactly like I remembered it before the war."

"Sometimes things change, even when we don't want them to," Keith whispered as the wind picked up. "I just hope you're not one of them." Carol smiled.

CHAPTER 6

Carol Falls in Love

Timeframe Clarification Here

KEITH MADE CAROL a part of his own family, bringing her with him every time he went home. Carol would stay in the guest bedroom upstairs and Keith would sleep in his room on the main floor.

With time, both Carol and Keith felt as if they were truly coming home whenever they visited. The blessing of meeting Keith became the blessing of being part of his family.

As she packed her clothes for one of these much-anticipated trips, Carol came across a picture of her father. In the recesses of her mind, she remembered her Dad and when she'd last felt like she had a real family at home. Her dad would play peek-a-boo around her crib. She'd laugh; then, when he'd disappear, she would look and wait for him to reappear, her saucer eyes eager to glimpse his Cheshire grin. She remembered bedtime stories and "pony back rides" on his back. She remembered being called "Daddy's little princess."

She shook her head and sniffed the tears back, then looked back at the photo again. Then she blinked willingly and the first tear began to run down her cheek. She blinked again and another appeared, this one clinging to the corner of her eye. In his private world, Daddy had played peek-a-boo and hide-and-seek against himself for years, always in search of the dad who would make his daughter proud. He would never have given her anything but the very best—she had always been his princess, she suddenly realized; the apple of his eye; the one he simply refused to disappoint twice. "Daddy, you forgot to look inside me," she whispered through the tremors in each breath. "I forgive you, but you should have... looked into my eyes. You would have seen the best of yourself looking back at you. You suffered more than I ever could. You thought you lost yourself." She gazed at the photo for a long time, focusing on his eyes and knowing that the best parts of her were there, too. Finally, glancing at the clock and realizing she was already late to meet Keith, she stuffed the photo into her pocket address book and stowed the address book in her purse. "Come on, Daddy!" she said, the ghost of a grin creeping up her left cheek as she swung the purse over her right shoulder. "We're already late. And you're coming to meet my future in-laws."

--)==(O (O==(--

On the way home, while Keith dozed in the passenger seat, Carol remembered her first semester at UConn. She had written letters as often as she could. There were the weekly letters home, but the letters she loved to write were the ones to Kim.

Had it really been almost two years since her first letter to Kim from school? She remembered sitting under the little crabapple trees on the quad behind the dorm and scrawling on a sheet of notebook paper, *I really miss you. This is the first time we've been apart this long. The world is bigger when you try to find out how big it is. But don't worry; I'm fine. I just see schoolgirls on the bus every day. There's a stop near the edge of campus, and I see them getting out at their stop with handfuls of Good–n-Plenty or M&M's. It takes me back to those days.*

How's community college? It must be nice to be near home. You'd like it here, though. UConn has a beautiful campus. Hopefully, next year you'll transfer. (Hint, hint!) So keep your grades up.

The classes are challenging. Government, history, English, and art—all of them would be lethally boring without Keith. However, I did sign up for dance. It's a blast, and it's good exercise, unlike studying.

Keith, the young man I told you about, is in most of my classes. I met him in English. He's from Hot-lanta (wink). There was something so familiar about him, even though we'd never met before... and then it occurred to me the other day: he reminds me of my father. He's soft-spoken and he listens to me as if whatever I say is the most important thing in the world. We study every night and often sit up talking long after the homework is finished.

Come to think about it, we've been pretty inseparable. I like him a lot. He seems to like me as well. To everybody else we're probably boyfriend and girlfriend, but we haven't kissed or talked about it. On the weekends, we often go to the Friday night football game and a show on Saturday night. He holds my hand and holds the door, walks on the street side of the sidewalk, and pushes in my chair for me. It makes me think of the things Dad used to do for Mom back before Vietnam.

Well, I still need to write my Mom tonight. So, call me on Sunday. It's your turn to call. Do not forget! (It's all love, sis.)

Carol

She used to write to Kim and Mom in the same sitting because she could send the letters at the same time. It was always hard to write to Mom after writing to Kim, but she never wanted to write to Kim after writing to Mom—that would only have made her sound angry and annoyed at Kim, which she wasn't.

She used to poke her cheek with the clicker end of the pen and try to think about what to say to Mom. Kim still lived next door to Mom and Ralph, but writing to the two different sides of that house was like writing in two different languages. Finally, she'd relent and write a very safe note to her mother:

Hi, Mom,

Hope you are well.

I'm doing fine and keeping my grades up in school. It's really safe here at UConn.

I'll send some more pictures of the campus.

I'll send my report card when it comes out.

I'll write soon.

Carol

As the ribbon of road started twisted and turned, Carol sighed. Her relationship with her mother was one thing that hadn't changed much since the fall of her freshman year.

She hated that her relationship with her mother was so weird, but she couldn't help it. Josephine and Ralph were married, and they wanted to keep it that way. And that was easy enough for them; their relationship appeared fine, with the help of an occasional blind eye. That was her mother's choice. Carol's knuckles clenched around the steering wheel at the thought of it all, though. "I will never forsake my daughter," she half-whispered, half-growled. "Never." Keith stirred a little, and then relaxed again, gently leaning with the countour of the road.

CHAPTER 7

Senior Year

Four Years Later

Dear Carol,

My sweet daughter, we've had our differences. Despite all that, it's time to bury the hatchet. You're in the fourth year of school and you never came home to check on your own mother, not once. It seems to me you could have gone to a college closer to home, like Kim did. Anyhow, that's water under the bridge now.

Kim mentioned that because of her graduation this month, she will not be able to attend yours. Ralph and I don't even know the date, let alone when, or where our tickets are.

May I remind you, we are family! I'm now your only family, as I recall. You are my only child. And I'm getting older.

Your stepfather, Ralph, wants to come to your graduation. Don't you think it's time to kiss and make up? He really does care about you. After all, he did help pay for your college room and board expenses.

Carol, you've not called us on Sunday night in a really long time.

Time is moving faster these days. We just want to hear from you and know you're well.

Write soon.

Love,

Mom

P.S. You know I love you. Do call this Sunday, won't you?

CAROL'S FACE WENT hard as a bucket of nails. Her eyebrows knitted together. Keith hovered a hand over her knee.

"What's wrong?" he asked. "Baby, I know you never want to talk about home, and I don't mean to pry, but it hurts me to see you like this."

Carol glanced toward Keith. Her faced softened for a moment when she saw his. Then she shook her head with a tiny, decisive motion. She embraced Keith's waist and laid her head on his chest. She was glad his family would be at her graduation. She closed her eyes and remembered when Keith had asked her to come home with him for break. She had laughed at him. "So you're just gonna show up with me," she needled him, "like, 'well, well, look what the cat dragged in!'" He'd let it go at the time, smiling coyly and saying, "Yeah, aight, that's right, that's what they'll say."

The very next day, the common phone in the dorm lounge had rung. Katie from down the hall had hollered until Carol ran up, hushing her. "Who is it?" Carol had mouthed. "Gwen Davidson," Katie had said matter-of-factly.

"Carol," she'd said, "I'm Gwen Davidson, Keith's mom. I hope he told you to expect my call. Now don't mind me getting straight to business here, but I simply cannot wait to meet you. You'll be joining us during the upcoming school break, I understand."

"Uh, well, yes, I mean Keith invited me…" Carol said, verbally stumbling along. "…that is, I thought, well, if it were all right with you, and—"

"Carol, you are always welcome with us. If you're dear to Keith, you're dear to us, too. You'll have the guest room. Are you allergic to anything?"

"No, nothing," replied Carol, letting the realization wash over her. Suddenly, a little click preceded a trombone-like voice. "Miss Carol," it said, "I'm Major Kevin Davidson, Keith's father."

"Pleased to meet you, sir!" she said, smiling uncontrollably.

"Not to get stuck on the technicality, but we actually haven't met yet—but I am very much looking forward to it. You are all Keith talks about, and I think it's wonderful he's found such a good friend."

After a whirlwind week of finals and preparations, Carol and Keith had arrived in front of the stately brick house at 5236 Forest Drive.

Carol was so excited to meet his parents, not to mention to get away from the school. The visit was everything she'd imagined and more.

After dinner on Saturday night, the entire family brought out their instruments and gathered in the sitting room to jam. The brothers switched instruments for different songs, rotating among the piano, drums, flute, guitar, mandolin, and tuba. Even their little girl, Leigh, played the tambourine.

Carol smiled.

"You doing better, babe?" Keith asked.

"Oh, yeah," she said mildly, closing her eyes again.

By her senior year, Carol had been to Keith's parents' home many times. They returned one final time before graduation. His parents promised to be there for graduation. His brothers and their wives and his young sister would also attend. Although the auditorium tickets were limited, Carol was able to donate her three allotted family tickets to the Davidsons. The family had decided those who couldn't get inside the auditorium would meet the rest of the family for dinner at a local restaurant after the ceremony. Everyone was excited for Keith and for Carol, who was the class valedictorian.

"Are you sure you don't want your mother to see you graduate?" Keith's mother asked after dinner one night. "Especially since you are the class valedictorian?"

Carol just shook her head. The room became silent. She remained quiet, so Keith's mother stopped pushing the issue.

"Well, we will cheer extra loud for you."

The family bought bouquets of red roses for both Carol and Keith. They kept their cameras flashing as the two walked across the stage and received their diplomas. After the ceremony, they went to a fancy seafood smorgasbord restaurant. Everyone shared from giant platters of lobster, shrimp, oysters, and giant crab legs.

The party was so loud, the restaurant owners had to hush them several times. The owners brought out a chocolate cake, with icing in white and purple lettering. "Congratulations, Keith and Carol! We're proud of you. Love, Your Family."

When everyone had eaten their desserts, Keith made an announcement. "Carol and I have decided to stay in Connecticut. We will be getting married soon, but for the time being, we will get different jobs and separate apartments."

"Are you sure?" Gwen asked, looking unsettled. She hadn't even seemed as upset over the high bill as she was over the fact that the young couple wasn't moving to Georgia.

"It would be nice if you moved back to Atlanta and be near the family." His father sounded sincere.

"No," Keith said adamantly. "We want to be on our own. Our minds are made up. We love you dearly and we'll visit as much as we can, but we have connections here, Carol's teaching certificate is good in Connecticut, and I've been studying Connecticut statutory law. Right now, it makes sense."

"I see you're keeping your head in the game," Kevin said with a note of approval. "And you know there's always room for you near Atlanta." The family raised their glasses for one final toast.

Later, Keith and Carol decide to move in together. They didn't tell Keith's parents, and they agreed to give vague answers whenever someone asked where Carol was living.

CHAPTER 8

Keith and Carol's First Apartment

New Haven, Connecticut; June 1986

"WHAT ARE YOU doing, Babe?" Keith walked into the bedroom and found Carol slipping some of the glossy-colored pictures taken at their graduation into an envelope with what looked like a letter.

She puffed a short, resigned sigh. "I just wrote my mother."

Dear Mom,

Graduation went smoothly. I am enclosing pictures so you can see what a good time we had. I just didn't want any bad memories on my special day, and I had none. This was one of the happiest days of my life. I hope to find a job soon. I will be staying in New Haven, Connecticut. I won't be moving back to Darlington.

Carol

She smoothed down the flap and bent down the tabs on the legal-sized manila envelope and set it aside.

As it turned out, Keith and Carol had found it much cheaper to live together. They just didn't want to tell their parents they were living in sin. They knew they would eventually get married.

They'd found the apartment for a reasonable price, which helped convince them to share it. "We'd each be paying more than that every month to have separate places," Carol had whispered to Keith.

They still had one more trip to make to the dorm to get the remainder of their things. She looked around their first apartment, happy to officially have her first "real place." She finally felt at home.

Home… she reflected on that word. It was something she hadn't felt since her father's death. Maybe it was that Keith was there; a man she could trust.

She tensed up as she suddenly remembered the morning when she woke up and found her stepfather, Ralph, in bed with her. Her mother had already left for work, and she had tried to jump up, but he had grabbed her by the waist and pulled her back and… she had cried and wailed as he moaned and grunted. Afterward, she scrambled away, then darted back and spat on him and croaked, "I will tell my mother, and you'll have to do that to someone in jail. If they're not doing it to you first." Ralph never came into her room again.

Three years later, Carol finally told her mother. Josephine didn't believe her. Nonetheless, Josephine confronted Ralph.

"She's lying, Josephine," Ralph said in a cautioning tone. He turned and gazed out the window. "You know," he said just loudly enough for Carol and Josephine to overhear, "I knew she never liked me. Not since day one." He pointed at Carol. "You're a foul liar for this," he said, shaking his head. "Jealousy ain't no reason to say nothin' like that." He turned to Josephine. "She probably just wants you to put me out."

"I'm not lying," Carol protested.

Her mother just looked back and forth from Carol to Ralph, then she shook her head and walked out of the room.

She never took Carol for a medical examination or counseling, and when the topic came up, Josephine would get very quiet. Carol vowed to herself that when she turned eighteen, she would never return home, not even once.

A cloud of doubt and suspicion hung over the house until Carol moved away to UConn. Ralph kept his distance and only spoke through Josephine if he had to relay a message to Carol. At mealtimes, Carol would just take her meal and eat in her bedroom. Everything she did in the room became another cog in the works of achieving her goal of moving out for good. She filled out all of her college papers alone at her desk. She studied for the SAT and also read the score report in her room—the one that told her she'd gotten a 1540 and won a scholarship. She jumped up and down as quietly as she could and screamed into her pillow so that nobody else would know that she'd accomplished her main goal: to go to the University of Connecticut School of Education.

She blinked, and Carol realized she was still standing in the sparsely furnished apartment. She went to the bathroom and checked her hair and makeup, and then grabbed the rental truck key.

Keith had been talking with one of the neighbors. She tapped him on the shoulder and he fell into step with her. They walked to the ground level and drove the U-Haul back to Carol's dorm to get the remaining items she had left in her old room. Then they visited Keith's dorm to get a few pieces he'd left behind as well.

Katie came by Carol's room to say her goodbyes. After they hugged, Carol gave her the large manila envelope. "Could you put this in the mailbox?" Katie nodded and took the letter. Her own family was waiting outside to take her to lunch.

As they were about to leave with the last of Carol's bags, another classmate, Nyema, called down the stairs.

"Carol, you have a phone call."

Carol turned around to go back up the stairs. "I'll meet you at the van," she called over her shoulder to Keith.

Carol bounced up the stairs and grabbed the pay phone that was swinging on its cord. "Hello," she said breathlessly.

Her heart almost stopped when she recognized her stepfather's voice. She could almost smell the whiskey on it through the phone. "I hope you can live with yo'self," he twanged like a cheap banjo, "Because you are the reason for your mother's death."

"What are you talking about?" Carol snapped, suddenly realizing that she wished she had slammed the receiver back into the cradle as hard as she could.

"Your mother is dead," Ralph repeated. "An' I hope you can live with yo'self, because you are the reason."

"What do you mean, 'the reason?'" Carol tried to let the anger lead, but she could feel her stomach and throat clench.

"Ever since your mother read that letter saying that you didn't want her at your graduation, she cried and worried herself right into this heart attack she had here today. Now, her death is on your hands for the rest of your life."

"No," she whispered.

"Whachasay? Speak up."

"Not. Just. Mine," Carol hissed. "Yours too."

She half-growled, half-screamed as she pounded the receiver down. In a flurry of sprite steps, she fled back into her empty dorm room and locked the door.

Katie saw her fly past the stairwell and raced back up to Carol's room. "What's the matter?" Katie cried out, pounding on the door. Soon a group of other young women gathered outside her door. They all began to chime in with worry.

"Let us in, Carol!"

"Are you all right?"

"Someone go get Keith," Nyema ordered.

Katie ran down the stairs to get Keith, and brought him back, yelling "Male on the floor!" as loudly as she could all the way up.

Keith took the steps two at a time. Once on the landing, he cried out, "Carol, what's wrong, baby? Please open up." He had no idea what was going on.

Finally, thirty long seconds later, the lock clicked and a sliver of Carol's face appeared.

Slowly, the door opened. Carol fell into Keith's arms. She sobbed continuously at first, and he couldn't understand what she was saying. At last, he deduced what had happened. "God, baby," he said, wrapping his sinewy arms around her. "This was not your fault. The only reason your stepfather is trying to put the blame on you is because he is trying to make you feel bad for what he did to you. Remember, the wrong was done to you, not the other way around."

Keith knew once he got Carol settled down and she had stopped crying, that she was in no condition to drive his car while he drove the U-Haul. So, he went to the office and told them what happened and they gave them permission to take as much time as they needed to leave. Keith and Carol stayed at the dorm that night, then left the next morning, glad to finally return to their new apartment in New Haven.

→→■◎ ◎■←←

They hadn't fully unpacked and organized the apartment before they went south for Josephine's funeral. One day after they'd gotten the news, they prepared for the twelve-hour drive.

As they packed, Keith turned to Carol. "Remember, baby, I'll be at your side—or very close by; whatever you need."

Carol's sighed and smiled wistfully through a furrowed face as she kissed him on the cheek. "Thank you so much for coming with me."

"Wouldn't have it any other way," he said softly. "I would never send you to fight the demons of your past alone." He squeezed her hand gently and she did the same in return.

⇒ ⇐

When they arrived in Darlington, Keith and Carol checked into the old Raceway Inn on Washington Street. They'd made sure to avoid mentioning where they'd be staying; in fact, they hadn't told anyone they were coming. Nobody needed further details.

Of course, Kim called not twenty minutes after they'd arrived. Carol smiled as she picked the bakelite receiver up at an angle. The telephone's bell *tinged* lightly and Carol felt better about the journey. Within moments, Kim was on her way over.

When Carol opened the door, she saw Kim's face hiding behind a large bouquet of tiger lilies and calla lilies. Somehow, in her other kitchen-mitted hand, Kim was balancing two trays of hot food separated by a pair of potholders.

After Keith ate, he took a walk around the motel grounds so that Kim and Carol could talk. Kim's smiles slowly faded into a firm, resolved game face.

"Ralph has told all your relatives and friends that you were the cause of your mom's heart attack, and he went out of his way to mention how you didn't even invite her to your graduation."

Carol's pupils narrowed and her nostrils flared.

"Kim, you are the only one I told about the rape. Once again, he's using me. And this time it doesn't matter what Mom would think!"

"Girl, there ain't good answers for this, but getting mad at him ain't even close. But don't worry; everybody knows Ralph is hitting the bottle real hard these days. That's all they need to know." Kim's arm snaked across Carol's back. "We can do this."

Carol's back hunched as she sobbed softly and leaned into Kim's arms. "She's gone," she whimpered several times.

As her breaths came and went unevenly, Carol smelled Kim's Chanel perfume and felt the tips of her hair tickling her teary cheeks. Slowly, her lungs relaxed and found their natural pattern again.

CHAPTER 9

Josephine's Funeral

The Next Day

WHEN CAROL AND Keith arrived at First Baptist Ebenezer, all heads turned. Carol almost wanted to turn and run, but she clamped down with iron force on Keith's left hand, pursed her lips, and blinked. Without breaking stride, Keith's chin dropped and head turned. He whispered in her ear, "Now you see why I liked the idea of the veil." She smiled a little bit, remembering that the fine black fabric gave her a measure of privacy she wasn't used to having. "And, baby," Keith added, "you're going to buy me a new left hand after we're done here, ain't that right?" She relaxed her grip and tried to shoot Keith a look, which—she suddenly realized—was really futile with the veil on. Suddenly, though, she felt herself stop fighting the adrenaline, and a sly smile crept across her face. She found herself concentrating on walking very quietly and simply. Halfway down the aisle, she angled closer to Keith. Their hips brushed, and then their legs fell into step together as they finished the trip to the front row.

As they entered the pew, the overwhelming smell of chrysanthemums reminded her of her father's funeral and without warning her knees buckled. Keith deftly let go of her hand, looped his arm through hers, and held her up as if nothing had happened. As she felt the wooden bench beneath her, Carol couldn't decide if she wanted to remember the moment forever or forget everything about the times she'd worn black in Ebenezer's sanctuary. The sheer veil tumbled over the edges of the fine-woven, wide-brimmed black hat and ended just high enough to showcase the pearl necklace above the neckline of an unusually well-tailored Vera Wang pencil dress that ended just below the knee. Keith's mother, of course, had sent it with a handwritten note. The shoes, simple but supple Italian leather heels, had arrived in the same box. How right Gwen had been, Carol thought, to say that comfortable shoes were the one thing everyone going to a funeral needs but nobody remembers. And they were comfortable! But even they couldn't match Keith's poise.

She leaned mildly, turned, and whispered in his ear, "Do not leave my side."

"Never," he whispered back as he held her hand closer.

"You okay?" Kim mouthed discreetly from a few feet away. Keith's jaw protruded a little and his eyes smiled as he nodded back. Kim gave a tiny nod. She whispered something to Ms. Penny and Ms. Penny nodded subtly as well.

Reverend Austin officiated in his usual way, and Carol heard more tones than words. Had it really been years since she'd listened to him eulogize her father?

And had that been so many years after the two of them had played in the garden? She remembered days when the garden was fertile, well worked, and weed free, bursting with vegetables, sweet tomatoes, carrots, greens, lettuce, and herbs. There was always more than enough to share with Kim and her family.

When had the garden lapsed into fallow ground, overgrown and untended? When did the fruit and vegetables rot on the vines? Was it before or after Mitch's death? Or was it during those days of quiet addiction?

Carol never once made eye contact with Ralph. Even when Keith escorted Carol to the casket to finally view her mother's remains, she never looked at him, but she could hear him sobbing uncontrollably. *Drunkard. Showman. Freeloader. Pretender. Child predator.* It took all her strength to keep from turning around and spitting out, "Hypocrite!" Keith's hand brushed her thigh almost imperceptibly and she drew a quick breath, returning to the moment and leaning into the crook of his arm.

At the graveside, Reverend Austin intoned the twenty-third Psalm in his gravelly baritone, "Thou preparest a table before me in the presence of my enemies; thou annointest my head with oil; my cup runneth over. Surely goodness and mercy shall follow me all the days of my life and I shall dwell in the house of the Lord forever."

"Amen," the community answered.

People began to put roses on the casket, as it was lowered on the bier.

She saw herself in the baby bath in the kitchen sink, and then Josephine picked her up and dried little Carol, who giggled and nosed her mother's breasts. Josephine sat and breast-fed baby Carol, and when she was full and slipping off to sleep, Josephine sang low and sweet, *"Hush, little baby, don't you cry..."*

Carol's loud sniffle cut the air clearly. Kim and her family all reached out to touch her shoulders, and Keith wrapped his arm around her.

Then, from behind them, Ralph bellowed, "There is no need for your crying now. You put her there!" Immediately a curtain of family and friends formed between Ralph and Carol.

Carol scurried awkwardly away, her heels kicking up tiny divots as she tried to balance and run through the grass back to the car. Keith pushed his Ray Bans onto his forehead and fixed his clear eyes on Ralph. "You are one sick individual," he said calmly. "If only everyone knew the real story!"

Ralph wrenched through the people between him and Keith, but when he tried to cock back and land the first punch, his nerve evaporated. Suddenly he looked unstable, and staggered a few paces to the side.

"Yeah," Keith murmured, pulling alongside Ralph, "You're not such a badass when you're looking at a real man instead of a little girl, huh?"

Ralph looked around to make sure none of his relatives or neighbors heard. A small gaggle of them had followed Carol, some were watching him and Keith but hadn't been close enough to overhear, and a few were drifting toward the zigzagging trail of cars lining the cemetery road.

As it had arrived, the motorcade eventually moved to and through the wrought iron gates and back out into the maze of streets and the rhythm of traffic lights.

CHAPTER 10

Young Love

The Next Day

THE NEXT MORNING Carol and Keith said goodbye to Kim and drove north once again. A few weeks later, after Carol and Keith settled in their new apartment, Carol went to Wilbur Cross High School and put in an application. Many teachers were retiring, and she impressed the English department chair with her interview.

Carol tried to convince Keith to substitute teach until the firefighters' civil service exam. Keith was hesitant because he did not want to get too invested to the kids and then have to leave. He decided to volunteer at the local firehouse until the test date came around. They had some savings, he reminded Carol, and if the test date was too far out, he would find a different job near the apartment.

One night, a couple of weeks before it was time for Carol to start school, while she and Keith were asleep, Carol began tossing and turning. She woke up screaming. By then, Keith had grabbed her. "Hush, babe. It is only a bad dream. I'm right here."

Carol hugged Keith tightly and burst out crying.

"What's the matter? What did you see?"

"I saw my mother," Carol whispered. "She was begging me to let her come to graduation. Meantime, my stepfather was raping me over and over, and she would not do anything to stop him."

"Shhh. Shhh." Keith patted her back.

Carol could not sleep the rest of the night, so Keith stayed up with her.

After that night, the bad dreams happened more and more frequently. Carol could never go back to sleep after one of the dreams, so she would struggle through the following day at work.

After several months, Keith talked about it with Carol. He waited for one of the rare mornings after she'd actually slept through the night. He handed her coffee to her in her favorite mug.

"Thanks," she said with a smile.

"Babe, pardon me for jumping right into this, but we need to see a doctor," Keith said. "I tried to wait a while, you know, hoping that the dreams would get less frequent. But it's been affecting you, and now it's affecting me too."

"What kind of doctor?" Carol asked with a little edge. In her town, you didn't visit a psychologist unless there wasn't even one family member or friend who would listen. A piece of her father rose up in her, and before she realized it, her eyes narrowed and she declared, "Because if you're saying I'm crazy or about to go crazy, well, I am neither."

Keith's face hardened and he looked away. He sipped from his mug and finally said, quietly, "I wish I knew how to help you, babe. I just don't know how to do it, though. I stay up with you when I can. But these days I find myself getting angry at you, but it's not even your fault. You don't want to stay up all night for no reason any more than I do. So either you need to see someone who can help you, or we both need to see someone who can help us."

Carol sipped pensively. "No drugs, right?"

Keith's eyes met hers quickly. "Drugs? No! No drugs. Not unless you're okay with it."

Tiny tears formed in the corner of Carol's eyes. "Thank you," she said, putting down the mug.

Carol saw a psychologist for several months. Her primary care physician had prescribed sedatives, but Carol kept the tiny paper folded in her purse.

Not long after that, Keith finally received the letter he was waiting for: the New Haven Civil Service Exam schedule. He qualified easily and, with the connections he'd made by volunteering at the firehouse, had all the support he needed for his application to the department. He wrote "Academy Training" in big red letters across six weeks of calendar days.

CHAPTER 11

A Surprise

One Year Later; New Haven Fire Department

"KEITH! TELEPHONE. IT'S CAROL!" A fellow fireman, Brad, a tall white man in his thirties, called from the fire station's kitchen.

Keith rushed to the kitchen, and grabbed the cordless phone from his co-worker. Because they worked together three days and two nights, the fire department was Keith's second family, and Brad was a stepbrother. He and the other firemen all knew that Keith and Carol lived together and were a serious couple.

"Baby, are you okay?" His heart was galloping in his chest. He knew Carol had gone for her yearly physical so he was afraid she'd had a bad report.

"Are you sitting down?" Carol asked mysteriously.

"What's going on?"

"I had to give a urine test at the doctor today."

"And—?"

"I thought we were protected. I used the foam according to the directions on the box. Anyhow," she paused for dramatic effect. "I'm pregnant. I'm sorry—I didn't mean to..."

"Hey, what do you mean, you're sorry? This is amazing! You are the best thing that ever happened to me! Yo, fellas!" Keith hollered as he high-stepped into the next room, holding the cordless phone like a championship trophy, "Guess what the most wonderful woman in the world just told me!?" He was greeted with whoops and hoots of joy, and he ran all through the station, raising his fist in the air like John Carlos at the '68 Olympics.

Whenever someone ran in from another room, Keith would playfully jab a forefinger into one of their buttons and say, "I'm'a be a daddy!"

"Congrats!" "My boy!" "New dad in the house!" Shouts echoed from every room.

Finally Keith realized he hadn't said anything to Carol in three minutes. "Uh, babe?" he said sheepishly into the receiver, pressing his mouth against it.

"Oh, there he is, Mr. New Dad!" Carol said, unable to hide the laughter in her voice.

"Thank you, baby—I was just kinda carried away for a second, you see— but, you heard, right? You heard how everyone's so happy for us?"

"As long as *you* are happy! You know, I'm getting more excited myself. Might be the best mistake I ever made! What do you think about making one of the bedrooms into a nursery?"

"Can we make it a fire station theme?" Keith asked giddily.

⟶▬◉ ◉▬⟵

Later, when Keith got off work, he stopped at Gilden's Jewelry and picked out a one-carat diamond ring. When he arrived home, he found Carol, who had just come home from school, still sitting in her car in the driveway. She seemed so young and alive—her hair shone in the sunlight like a raven's wing. Her mahogany skin radiated its own warm as she stepped out of the car and beamed at him.

"Come take a ride with me, Li'l Mama," he said. He reached down and rubbed Carol's flat stomach with pride.

"Why? Where we going?"

"I left my wallet in the station. You are looking so good, I can see the difference already."

Carol blushed. Then she let out a deep yawn. "I'm kinda sleepy, but I'll ride with you."

"No wonder you've been sleeping so much. Is that why you threw up the other morning?"

"Yes." She nodded sheepishly. They both shared a conspiratorial grin.

Within twenty minutes, they pulled into the station. Keith's shift was just ending, but everyone from his crew was still there, and the new shift was just arriving. Almost every fireman in the unit was in the locker room. Keith dared

Carol to go in and act as if she were looking for Keith but couldn't find him. She grinned again. Free access to the locker room at a fire station? She tried to suppress her smile as she pushed open the door. But before she could say something about looking for Keith and asking if anyone had seen him, she saw they were all grinning right at her. Conversation had stopped, and she turned around.

Keith was on his knee, framed in the doorway, right in front of Carol and all his co-workers. He ferreted the small box out of his pocket and took out the ring. Carol gasped at the size of the rock as he cradled her left hand with his right. "Carol, will you marry me?"

Tears sprung into her eyes. "Yes, baby," she cried, kissing him. Keith pushed the ring onto her finger, grabbed her up in his arms, and kissed her as he slowly spun. His face got wet from all tears rolling down her face.

The locker room exploded in cheers.

Brad pushed through the crowd to the new fiancées. "Come to the kitchen," Brad directed the couple. They followed him down the hall and through another door.

"Congratulations!" the men shouted in unison. They blew party horns and threw confetti, then parted to reveal a long wooden table with a bucket of homemade ice cream and a beautiful sheet cake emblazoned, "Marry me, Carol!" in chocolate script.

CHAPTER 12

The Wedding

Time Identifier Here

KEITH COULDN'T HAVE been more aware that time was short to make preparations. They only had seven months to plan, host, and recover from what he hoped would be Carol's dream wedding. After all, his parents would never approve of having a baby outside marriage. The morning after the firehouse celebration, he and Carol decided to call Keith's parents.

They grinned at each other as they shared a receiver, his left ear and her right ear tickling each other. When Keith's mom and dad were both on the line, the young couple spoke as one.

"Mom, Dad, we're getting married!" they exclaimed.

"Great news!" Kevin said, voice full of approval.

Gwen began to gush with excitement. "Carol, you know other than our youngest, all I have are sons. You are the daughter I always wanted! And if you're okay with my help, I'd love to have the honor of helping you plan the wedding! Leigh is too young to get married just yet, so I thought I was going to have to wait a few more years, but this is wonderful!"

With tears rolling down her face, Carol answered, "Yes, yes! Thank you so much, Mom! With my mother gone, I really do appreciate it."

The following morning, Keith posted flyers at the fire station requesting a referral to a good real estate agent. It turned out that Johnny Blake, the rear ladder driver, was married to a Realtor.

"I want a three-bedroom house in a quiet neighborhood in a good school district," Keith told Simone Blake over the phone later that week.

Simone came back with about six addresses for Keith to look at. He didn't tell Carol because he wanted to surprise her.

Meantime, Carol was distracted by the generosity her soon-to-be in-laws lavished on her. They arranged the invitations, the venue, the flowers, and the catering arrangements, checking in with Carol every day to gather more information.

Keith's parents came to town; his mother helped Carol pick her wedding dress while Keith and his father went to check out the houses Simone had recommended. Keith was very partial to a three-bedroom colonial with two-and-a-half baths, a fireplace, and a full, finished basement with a lounge and a game room.

The house also featured a two-car garage. As Keith and his father drove away from the house at the end of the cul-de-sac in Hamden, Simone mentioned that Keith wouldn't even have to deal with a bidding process because the property was newly built.

A few days later, when Keith called Simone to ask about the details for submitting the down payment, Simone was confused. "The down payment already arrived," she said. "Yes, here it is. Yesterday."

Keith hesitated. "Really?" he asked.

"Your father brought it by for you," she said. "He didn't mention it?"

"No, he must have forgotten that he didn't tell me," Keith said. "Thanks so much!"

That night over dinner, Carol told the story of how she had discovered that her dress had been paid for. Keith smiled and shook his head in amazement. "Do I get to see it?" he asked.

"I suppose one peek won't hurt," Carol said, leading Keith to the bedroom closet. Keith smiled when he saw the simple A-line satin gown with its beaded bodice.

->==◉ ◉==<-

September 26 dawned crisp and cool but warmed up nicely as the early autumn day took shape. The New England sky was rich bluebird blue without a cloud in sight.

Carol gave a sigh of contentment as Gwen brushed her face with a soft dust of foundation and examined her work in the mirror over the dressing table.

"He's never seen you like this before!" Gwen whispered. "I guarantee it."

Keith knocked at the door. "Carol! Are you ready yet?"

"You get on back down the hall!" Gwen shot back. "No seeing the bride before Kevin walks her to your side."

Keith's entire family was present. Leigh, the flower girl, tossed white rose petals into the aisle. Walter, the eldest of Keith's brothers, was Best Man. Of course, Kim was Carol's Maid of Honor. She wore a lavender, floor-length gown. Her fiancé, Mike, had flown in and was her escort.

Kim's father gave Carol away. Kim's family, and some of Carol's teacher friends were there to support them.

The wedding was held at New Haven First Baptist, Keith and Carol's home church, a small traditionally Black congregation in East Rock.

In typically generous fashion, Gwen and Kevin had arranged the reception to be held at Keith and Carol's quaint white colonial in Hamden. Everyone, most especially Keith and Carol, marveled at the new modern furnishings that had been installed while they'd been away.

They tried to keep their gasps, oohs, and aahs to themselves as they noticed the burnt orange play pit sofa in the living room and the cherry wood sets in the bedrooms.

The backyard had become a bevy of tents under which guests could find food, custom blended drinks, a live band, a dance floor, and white tables covered with lavender tablecloths and classic folding wooden chairs. Carol was in her glory. When she and Keith danced a slow dance, their first dance as a married couple, there wasn't a dry eye in the house. The two danced like practiced partners with years of experience. Everyone ate, drank, laughed and danced the rest of the night away. They did the Soul Train until everyone was exhausted.

When the celebration wound down, Kim's family and Keith's family went back to the hotel and gathered up their belongings for their flights back home the next day. Kim stayed behind to spend a few precious moments with her best friend.

Keith's friends from the station gave him envelopes with cash gifts and wide-shouldered hugs and firm pats on the back. "'Ey, don't even worry 'bout this mess," Rubin the mechanic said, gesturing toward the backyard. "Tomorrow I'm'a grab a few of the guys and come clean up. And I promise we won't knock on the door or look in the window, neither!" He and Keith broke into split watermelon grins.

Once the last of the firefighters had driven away, Keith went upstairs, drew a bath, and lit lavender candles while Carol and Kim reclined on the couch.

"You look so happy," Kim said.

"I am! But I wish my mother could have been here. I feel bad about what happened."

"Sister, it's like I been telling you: not. Your. Fault. That man who calls himself your stepfather smells like a distillery. He's been that way every day since your mother's death. Lost his job, too. He's still in the house, but it's falling apart. Your mother's insurance is all he has, and at this rate who knows how long that'll hold out."

"That no-good—" Carol caught herself. "I don't care what happens to him. No, actually, I do. I hope he dies. I have my new family, and I don't ever want to look back. Please, Kim, as long as we're friends, and as long as I'm alive, don't ever mention him to me again."

Kim sipped the last of her champagne and put the flute down on the side table.

"Anyhow, I have a secret I want to tell you," Carol whispered.

"Mmm?" Kim's eyebrows perked up.

"I'm pregnant."

"What?"

"When a man and a woman really love each other, Kim, there's a special—"

Kim playfully swung her hand toward Carol's head and Carol drew back quickly, giggling. "I know *that*," Kim retorted playfully. I mean when are you due?"

"In about six months."

"You've been holding out on me!"

"No-one knew. Well, Keith's co-workers know. He's not much of a secret-keeper about that."

"His mom and dad, do they know?"

"Ironically, no. He hasn't brought it up to them. You know, we were going to get married anyway, and we're happy, and they'll be happy when we tell them."

"Girl, this is wonderful news! How are you feeling?"

"A little nauseous, but the doctor said that this is normal. I eat crackers for it. I already love my baby. I can't explain it. I feel like I can be the mother my mother was when my father was alive."

The two women hugged. Kim squeezed Carol the way she used to and then eased up quickly. "Sorry, li'l girl," she said sunnily, gently stroking Carol's belly. "Can't have your godmother squeezing you to death before you're even born."

CHAPTER 13

The First Baby
Two Days After the Wedding

KEITH AND CAROL went to the obstetrician's office together. Carol's ob-gyn visits had started eight weeks into the pregnancy, and so far she'd attended all the prior visits alone. They wanted to find out the sex of the baby together.

The doctor told them Carol was about twelve weeks along, and commented that it might be too soon to find out the sex of the baby yet. Keith and Carol were eager, though. They paid for an ultrasound, a new and optional procedure that showed a blurry black and white picture of the baby.

"It's a healthy boy!" the doctor announced.

Keith gave out a loud whoop of joy. He reached over and kissed Carol. "Thank you, baby!"

Carol began to cry. "No, thank you, baby!" She'd wanted to give Keith a son. He was such a good man that she wanted to see him raise another one.

After the appointment, giddy with excitement, they called Keith's parents. Gwen and Kevin didn't seem the least bit concerned that Carol had been pregnant when they got married.

Keith went to the firehouse. He handed out expensive cigars while everyone thumped him on the back and high-fived him. His co-workers all seemed happy for him. "Way to go, man!"

Keith went home and got to work on the "little man's" room. He pressed the decals of the fire station, the trucks, and tiny firemen onto the wall. He picked out a wooden rocking chair, baby toys, even a small football and other sports equipment. He bought maple wood furniture and an expensive crib with a canopy. He picked out many bold blue and red outfits. Keith finished the room in a few weeks' time. He wouldn't let Carol lift anything.

Carol worked up to her eighth month, at which point she couldn't tolerate standing on her feet in her classroom for long periods of time.

The first week Carol was off from work, she noticed minor chest pains. At first, they came and went quickly. She wrote it off to heartburn, which she'd had intermittently since college. She tried to ignore it as the pains lasted longer and got stronger, but she finally decided to call the doctor. During an ultrasound, the doctor noticed Carol had a slightly irregular heartbeat. Several times it started and stopped without any apparent cause. The doctor noted in her chart that he should monitor her heart during delivery. He did a vaginal exam to check the baby's position. "His head is in the birth canal. Your cervix is effaced to about one centimeter, so you could go in labor within the next two weeks. Just go home and put your feet up. But call 911 if your pain gets past five—that means you need an ambulance to bring you in and see a specialist. Tell them Yale New Haven Pediatric Cardiac unit if that happens, but in the meantime take it easy. I think hard work encourages these arrhythmic patterns."

As soon as she got home, Carol started feeling twinges in her lower back. She drank some warm milk, then took a short nap. She woke up with a sensation that she needed to have a bowel movement. When she went to the bathroom, she saw what her baby book had described as "the bloody show."

She called the firehouse right away. "Keith, I've had my bloody show. I went to the doctor today. Who would've thought I would go into labor now?"

"I thought you were not due until three more weeks," Keith exclaimed. He had planned to take two weeks off before her due date. "Okay, hang on a sec. I'll be there." He checked in with the chief, who called friends at the local police precinct. A two-car escort led Keith straight home, where he helped Carol into the car.

After admitting Carol at the maternity ward, two nurses rushed her to the labor room. Dr. Dais and another specialist were called in. They spoke in tense, hushed tones with each other before one of them took Keith aside. Pushing his reading glasses up onto his bald head, the specialist sighed. "Your wife's blood pressure is unusually high; dangerously high, really. I don't like having to tell you this, but you'll be lucky to leave here with both her and your baby." Keith sank against the wall and prayed while medical professionals hovered around Carol and attached monitors.

Carol's ob-gyn, Dr. Wilson, strode in moments later. "Prep her," she said determinedly. "We're a little behind on this." Keith popped up and took two steps toward Dr. Wilson, who explained quickly. "Carol has pre-eclampsia complications; specifically, toxemia. It's serious. I'm on my way to assist at the emergency C-section."

Keith felt tears fill his eyes. He pulled himself together, prayed hard, then trotted alongside Carol as her bed glided through the hallway. She could tell by the way the doctors were acting and the look on Keith's face that something was wrong. "Is my baby going to be all right?" She began crying. "I'm scared."

He kissed her. "Everything is going to be all right, baby. I'm going to stay with you. Baby needs a C-section, okay?"

Carol squeezed Keith's hand. "Okay," she said. "Whatever Baby needs."

An hour later, three doctors emerged from the surgical unit. One was holding a tiny, tightly bundled six pound eight ounce little girl.

After letting Keith hold and kiss his little girl, a nurse whisked the little baby off to intensive care. Keith collapsed in Carol's recovery room before she even arrived. Later that evening, he woke to hear a familiar voice. "Keith?"

He sat up and let his eyes adjust to the low light. "Carol, babe," he said, finding her hand. "Is he doing all right?" she asked.

"She," he gently corrected. "And yes, she's doing okay. She's like her mom; she's a fighter who beat some serious odds today."

Carol squinted. "What odds?"

"You and the baby could have died because you had toxemia, but I decided to believe that you both would be okay. I was scared, but you didn't need to be scared too."

"Come here," Carol said. "I mean, good thing I'm slim again..." she shifted slowly to one side of the bed and Keith crawled under the cover beside her. "They'll kill us if they find us cuddling on the fresh stitches," Carol whispered. "Where's the incision?" Keith asked. "Over here," she said, guiding his hand over her abdomen. "So don't touch it or lean on it." Keith smiled. "Don't you worry; I'll stay on this side." Carol lay on her back and Keith lay on his side, his chin on Carol's shoulder and his hand on her arm. They slept until morning.

During Carol's two–day stay, the doctors told the young couple that if she was to have any more kids, there would be a good chance that neither Carol nor the baby would survive.

"Why don't you let us do a tubal ligation?" Dr. Wilson asked.

Carol hesitated. She was only twenty-four. She didn't want to risk death once more, but she didn't want to say no to other children. What about a boy?

"How about the pill?"

"Carol, missing a pill could be a matter of life and death."

"Okay, how about the Depo-Provera shot?" Carol asked. She had just read in a magazine about a newly approved birth control shot you could take every three months.

"Well, that makes me a little more comfortable," Dr. Wilson said, clearly relieved as she scribbled on her prescription pad.

Keith closed his eyes and thanked God for his wife and daughter.

->==0 0==<-

Carol recovered well. She kept up with all her appointments and faithfully got her Depo shot. The doctor told Keith her shot schedule and he reminded her, too.

Eight weeks after she'd first left work to have and take care of the baby, Carol returned to teaching. Keith's schedule at the firehouse gave him three days on followed three days off, so Keith and Carol hired a nanny two days per week.

Baby Kalley smiled whenever she saw Keith's or Carol's face. She loved reaching for her parents' hands, playing peek-a-boo, and riding in the baby sling. Keith and Carol would talk to Kalley while they walked, cooked, and cleaned. They would read to her often, too.

One afternoon, Carol peeked into the room that Keith had prepared. On top of a stack of unopened toys sat a battery-powered fire truck. Kalley had plenty of toys in her room, but perhaps Keith had given the little fire truck to Kalley anyway. She pressed the lights, and they flashed and the truck's siren wailed.

"Fire team to the rescue!" announced a recording. Carol's eyes welled up and she prayed for a son. "Dear God," she whispered, "Deliver me and my babies." She knew the risks, but felt compelled to try once more to bear a son.

Just a month and a half before Kalley's first birthday, Kim's and Keith's families were on their way to New Haven for Kalley's christening. Kim was excited; she'd be the godmother. Everyone couldn't wait to hold and see Kalley for the first time instead of trying to envision themselves in photographs.

About a week before everyone arrived for the christening, Carol had a Depo shot appointment. When she arrived at the medical office, she noticed a new doctor was on duty.

"I won't be taking another Depo shot," she said matter-of-factly. "Too much weight gain. I'm going to try the traditional birth control pills." Too much weight gain wasn't the only thing; the Depo shot had really killed her sex drive. She kept Keith happy, and she knew she should be feeling some tingles when he ran his hand along the back of her neck, but it just wasn't the same. Sure, she also dealt with some patches of irregular sleep, but that had never dulled her appetite in prior years.

The new doctor didn't introduce himself. He pulled out his pad and pen immediately. Without looking up, he remarked, "Well, the decision is yours." Had he even opened the chart? Carol wondered for a moment, but then stifled the question. Did she even want him to?

A day later, when Keith came home, he flopped down on the couch. "Whooee!" he sighed. "Just open up the windows and we'll roast marshmallows, girl."

Carol couldn't help but smirk. "I thought the blaze was on the Branford side."

"It was, and I guarantee it even made West Haven warmer. Took forever to get that thing under control, and now that poor house is the wettest hot mess in the county."

Carol was surprised but happy that Keith didn't ask about her doctor's appointment. She made herself busy preparing for the weekend, which brought with it the christening. After a few minutes, Keith got up and vacuumed the floors. Carol continued cooking, working on two recipes alternately.

They had bought Kalley a frilly white christening dress with matching peau de soie shoes with tiny little t-straps. Both Keith and Carol would wear matching navy suits.

Keith's family and Kim's family had flown in on Friday evening, the day before the christening. For the first time, their church family was able to meet their extended family. Keith's parents held and kissed the baby so much that Carol and Keith had to take Kalley out of their arms to continue the ceremony.

"Oh, she's just so sweet. I wish I could keep her," Gwen cooed as she reluctantly handed over the baby.

With tears in her eyes, Kim looked on, as she stood up as godmother. Charles, one of Keith's friends from the station house, stood up as godfather.

After the ceremony, back at the house, Kim pulled Carol to the side.

"Girl, you know I love my niece. She is beautiful."

"Thank you. You've been sending her too many clothes."

"Don't even think about it. Anyhow, you've got a beautiful family. You've got a beautiful daughter. I know you wanted to give Keith a son, but he seems happy with his little girl."

Carol didn't answer. She averted her gaze. She still wanted to give Keith a son more than anything. How could Kim know already?

"What do you mean?" Carol asked suspiciously.

"Let me say this as delicately as possible. I heard about how you're not supposed to get pregnant again. You've got your family, and they need you. Carol, please don't take a chance and gamble with your life. That's all I'm saying. I know you never said anything like that, etcetera, etcetera, but Carol, I know you. I know that you don't really let go of things. I love that about you, and this time it's got me a little scared."

Carol smiled and held up both hands in mock innocence. "I'm straight," she laughed, and she and Kim hugged. "No more babies." It tore Carol up to lie so boldly, but she wanted God alone to decide whether or not she'd have another baby, and at what price.

Everyone spent the night at the young Davidsons' house so they could spend more time with Kalley.

Gwen and Kevin fell in love with their granddaughter at more and more as Sunday waned. "Kalley is a good baby," Gwen commented. "She looks like her daddy at that age and she has a beautiful temperament. She seldom cries unless she's hungry or wet."

Kim and the family all left on Monday. Carol took the day off to say her goodbyes and spend the last few minutes with them.

That same week Carol's period came, and that following Sunday she never even touched her pills.

One evening, Keith looked up from dinner suddenly. "Did you go to your doctor's appointment?"

Carol nodded and hoped Keith didn't notice her surprise. He had remembered! "Uh huh." She felt a twinge of guilt because she had never lied to Keith. He'd forgive her when he held his son, she told herself.

"And?" he asked.

"As usual, babe. We're protected!"

Keith looked relieved as they both laughed.

CHAPTER 14

A Matter of Life or Death

Time Indicator Here

As TIME WENT by, the young couple became closer. Carol's libido returned and she enjoyed sex again. For their birthdays, Keith and Carol would celebrate by taking each other to dinner.

For Carol's upcoming birthday, however, Keith wanted to surprise her with something different; something special. He called two of Carol's girlfriends at Wilbur Cross, Jennifer and Dana, and asked them if they could keep Carol a couple of hours after school so that he could surprise her with a candlelit dinner. Her friends agreed. It would work seamlessly; since Keith was off from work that day, Carol wouldn't worry about rushing home to get the baby.

During the ruse, Dana stopped by the house and picked up Kalley for the evening. When Carol finally pulled up in the driveway, she wondered why her house looked so dark from the outside. Where was Keith?

When she stepped inside, she heard one of her favorite songs, Teddy Pendergrass' ballad, "Turn off the Lights," playing softly in the background. The only light flickering in the dining room came from rows of tiny tealight candles lining the table. Several silver chafing dishes covered what smelled like a combination of her all-time favorite foods: lobster, shrimp, steak, and baked potato. In the center of the table was a bottle of Dom Perignon and two champagne glasses.

"Oh, my God!" Carol whispered under her breath. "Keith?"

"I've got all your favorites, too," Keith replied, emerging from the kitchen carrying a cake with "For the Love of You" written in red icing. Red rose petals trailed from the table to the bedroom. Carol gasped as Keith stepped into the light, wearing a pair of black silk boxers, a black bow tie, and black patent leather shoes. "Look at you!" She smiled as brightly as she reached for Keith and kissed him passionately, until he made her let go.

"Slow down. I don't want to rush things. Save all of this for dessert." He glanced down at his bulging shorts.

Carol grinned and gave him a seductive smile. They sat down and began to slowly feed each other. They stared into each other's eyes the entire time.

Before they knew it, they finished eating. Suddenly, Carol jumped up from her seat. "Wait—where's Kalley?"

Keith pulled his finger to his lips. "Shh. Tonight is yours. The baby is with Dana. That's why she left your gathering early."

"Oh!" Carol said, steadying herself on the chair. "Okay." Keith's hands traced the underside of her arms slowly from wrist to elbow, then around and up to the tops of her shoulders, and she turned to face him. Each undressed the other as they kissed and nibbled each other's necks gently. Soon their sighs became louder and longer, until Carol backed slowly out of the kitchen and down the hallway, the cool rose petals tickling the bottoms of her feet and guiding her to the bedroom. Keith followed, playfully and then slowly kissing and then licking lower and lower as Carol reclined on the bed.

Half an hour later, they lay side by side in each other's arms, spent. Their breathing slowed and their hearts cooled. As they spooned, they caressed each other and whispered their little phrases of affection to each other.

As Keith smoothed his hand over her stomach, he joked, "Girl, that meal went straight to your stomach!" As he rubbed over the area again, his forehead wrinkled a little.

"What do you mean?" Carol asked.

Suddenly, Keith sat up on his elbow and looked squarely at Carol. "Wait a minute." He looked down at her stomach, which swelled mildly, peaking at her navel. "You're pregnant! But... but you can't be pregnant, right? You can't be pregnant, can you? Tell me I'm wrong."

Tears instantly began to rush down Carol's face. "I'm so sorry."

Keith jumped out of the bed and threw on his clothes in furious movements, fussing the entire time. "What? Are you out of your mind? You know the doctor said another pregnancy could kill you! I don't want to even take the chance of losing you. And we talked about this! We agreed! What were you thinking?"

Carol continued crying. "I just wanted you to be happy. Don't you think I noticed the difference when the doctor told me that we were having a boy, and when we found out we had a girl? I just wanted to give you a son."

"How happy do you think I will be if something happens to you and the baby? What's going to happen to me and Kalley?"

Keith stomped into the kitchen and sat at the table, his face propped on his fist. His foot tapped hard and fast. He didn't know whether to be mad or to console her for being willing to risk her life to try to give him a son. He finally got his thoughts together, then trudged back into the bedroom.

He took a crying Carol into his arms, and caressed her back. "Baby, it's going to be all right." He reassured her through his own tears. They fell asleep in between relief and fear, with teardrops wetting both of their pillows.

They didn't discuss the matter for days or for weeks. Every time they were at home together, Keith wanted to ask her when was she going to schedule the abortion, but deep down inside he knew how badly she wanted the baby. Even surer than that, her mind was already made up.

Carol kept the company of her own thoughts often in those weeks. She avoided Keith whenever she could, to stave off the imminent conversation. She understood why it worried him, but her intuition told her that logic would have to take a long-awaited break.

Finally, one day, Keith saw her closing the door as he emerged from the bedroom. He rushed over and jammed his foot in the door, and then smiled, and put his finger through Carol's beltloop, pulling her back.

"I love you, baby," he said, kissing her gently on the cheek. "I see you trying to run off, and I know why—because I'm'a run after you and stick my foot in the door and put my finger through your beltloop and then pull you back toward me and tell you that I'm scared. And you might not want to hear that, and that might not be anything that needs to change, but you need to hear it because I need to say it. We just go around trying to pretend things are cool, and it's possible that they are cool, but we both still need to be real with each other. So, here it is: I am afraid of what will happen to me and Kalley if something happens to you."

He paused. "This situation is tearing me apart from the inside. Tell me what am I supposed to do."

Carol took his hand and put it on her stomach. The baby kicked. Without a word, he knew she was already too far along to even consider a medical procedure. "Just be behind me one hundred percent. Let's make this easier for both of us. We know there is a chance, but life is a chance. You must know there is nothing you can do to make me change my mind, but I do need you and God to be with me. I know I should have done this from the start, but now I need your support more than ever. I will die without it. But with it? I think we can do anything."

Keith bowed his head and began to pray. Carol nodded her head. "Lord, please protect our unborn child and Carol. In the name of Jesus."

"Amen." They both looked up with tears in their eyes.

Keith and Carol prayed over the situation daily, talked with their minister, and not announce the pregnancy until Carol began to show.

CHAPTER 15

The Blessing

Time Indicator Here

A FEW MONTHS later, one day, while she was standing at the chalkboard at work, Carol felt warm dampness between her legs. She put the chalk down and told her students to practice their spelling words. She went immediately to the teacher next door and asked her to watch her class while she went to the ladies' room. She saw a big glob of red in her panty liner. Her heart started pounding. She was no doctor, but she knew something was wrong. At only six and a half months pregnant, not quite twenty-eight weeks' gestation, she wasn't feeling any pain, but she wasn't supposed to bleed, either. As soon as she cleaned herself up, she called Keith from the teachers' lounge.

"Baby, I'm bleeding."

Keith sprang into action. "I'll be there to pick you up."

"No, meet me at the ER. I'm well enough to drive."

She let the principal know she had to leave early for an emergency, then drove to the Yale New Haven Emergency Room, twenty-five minutes away from her school.

Within minutes, Keith arrived. The doctors whisked her away in a wheelchair and into the emergency room. They did blood tests, a quick internal exam.

"We're going to have to admit you," the doctor on duty said urgently.

The test showed that Carol was hemorrhaging from a ruptured uterus. The doctor would have to deliver the baby early. This trouble, the physician explained, was called placenta previa. "And it's a good thing some of the bleed showed externally," he said to Carol. "You and your little girl were probably saved because of that."

Keith kissed Carol, and then the attending assistants moved her toward the surgical ward again. Keith waited in the waiting room, thinking and praying— but glad that the doctor had seemed so optimistic. Several hours later, a nurse emerged, smiling, to report that the baby and Carol were stable and recovering. Keith thanked God for another healthy baby and for Carol's safety.

That Sunday, Keith and Kalley went to church before going to visit Carol and the new baby. The pastor and the church members all said a prayer to bring them home safely.

"Lord, we trust you know what is best, but bring this young mother and wife and new baby home safely to her husband and other baby. Romans 8:28 says, 'And we know that in all things God works for the good of those who love him, who have been called according to his purpose.' We ask this in the name of Jesus. Amen."

"Amen." The entire congregation rejoined.

After a week, Carol was strong enough to be discharged from the hospital. She'd had the emergency delivery and a tubal ligation. The doctor prescribed heart medicine for Carol because the procedures had further weakened her heart.

Keith and Carol named the new baby Lisa. She had to stay in the hospital almost three months until she weighed five pounds; then, finally, they brought her home. Even though it seemed like forever during those three months in the hospital, with the daily visits first to the neonatal intensive care unit and then to the premature deliveries nursery, the days flew by once baby Lisa came home.

CHAPTER 16

A Moral Dilemma

Time Indicator Here

WITH KEITH AND Carol working, the girls running around the house together and getting into everything, and the cycle of birthdays and holidays, the years accelerated. The family still needed the nanny when Keith was at work, but that was still only two days a week. The girls' close ages made things easier; it wasn't hard to entertain both of them, to take them to the same places, or to read them the same books.

One Saturday at about eight in the evening, Carol, Keith, and the kids were in the family room watching a movie. The phone rang, and Keith answered it.

"Hello."

"Hey, Keith, it's Kim." She didn't quite sound like her usual self.

"Hi, Kim. Is everything all right?"

"Yes, I guess everything is okay. How are my godkids?"

"They're fine! Growing so fast I can't believe it. They are here watching TV with us. Looks like they've dozed off."

"Can I speak to Carol?"

"Sure!" Keith smiled as he handed the phone across the couch. "Carol, honey, it's Kim."

"Hey, girl! What's up?" Kim said. "I've been trying to figure out whether or not to call you."

Carol said, "Why? What's up?"

Kim cleared her throat. She began speaking slowly, reluctantly. "Well, I've been hanging out all day with my girlfriend from work. Mike told me your stepfather must have called at least ten times, talking about it being urgent for me to call him. When Mike gave me the number, it was a hospital number."

Carol hurried away into the kitchen. "And?"

Kim continued. "He explained to me that he only had a short time to live and he begged me to tell you how much he needed to apologize to you before leaving this world."

Carol felt her blood pressure rise, and her face pressed against her skull with frightening force. Almost mute with rage, she tried to stay quiet enough that she wouldn't scare the children. After a few seconds, she sputtered, "The sooner he dies, the better I'll feel, but until then, I don't want to hear anything he has to say. Since you are my best friend, you were supposed to tell him a thing or two because you knew how I feel about that situation. Not only that, I told you not to mention anything concerning him ever again. Now what kind of friend are you?"

"You're not wrong, Carol." Kim's voice wavered. "I'm sorry, but I was only trying to respect his last wishes before he goes."

Carol's voice went up another octave as she screamed, "I guess you did by disrespecting mine!" Carol threw the phone, which bounced off the wall and finally lay in the middle of the kitchen.

Keith rushed in. "What's up, babe?"

Once Carol explained what happened, Keith put his hands on her shoulders. "Take it easy, honey. Kim's your friend. How come you're taking it out on her?"

Carol pulled back and then rushed past Keith, yelling, "Why are you taking their side?" She ran into the bedroom and slammed the door with a resounding bang.

The loud voices woke the girls. They whined because they knew something was amiss. Keith went back to the living room and cuddled the girls and read them a book. "Mommy's gonna be all right," he told them. "She'll come in and kiss you later, but probably after you're asleep."

Keith knew how Carol needed her space. He took the girls to their room and put them in one twin bed together. Then he climbed into the other twin bed.

Carol sat on the bed and ping-ponged back and forth between sorrow and rage. She thought back to the days right after her father's death, and how her relationship with her mother had changed from the time she met Ralph. She'd asked Josephine about it several times.

"Mom, why don't you stop seeing Ralph? I liked it better when it was just you and me. I'm not his little girl; I'm yours. I don't like him; I love you."

"Honey, why don't you like him?" Her mother had asked.

"I don't like the way he makes me feel."

"Carol, I'm going to explain this to you and I hope you can understand. When your Dad died, our lives changed dramatically. First of all, I've had to work night and day to keep a roof over our head and food in our belly. I'm tired. Bone tired. Ralph said he doesn't want me working that hard. He wants to marry me."

"Mom, I don't like the way he looks at me. He makes my skin crawl."

"Baby girl, you're just imagining things 'cause he's not your Dad. I know how crazy you were about your Dad. But he's gone and we need the protection of a man in our life. It's too hard for a woman and child alone. He said he makes enough that if I don't want to work I don't have to."

"Mom, we're doing just fine. You and me. We don't need nobody else."

Carol remembered how she sobbed and begged, but after about six months, her mom married Ralph anyway.

"I want him to die," Carol whispered again and again, looking through the dusky grey near-dark in the bedroom. "The world will be a better place without him. He can go to hell and rot as far as I'm concerned."

As the minutes stretched on and Carol lay on the bed, she wondered why she'd said what she'd said to Kim. She was angry with Ralph—and that was an issue all its own. She fell asleep on top of the comforter, in her clothes, drifting in and out of snippets of dreams from her childhood.

The next day was Sunday, and the family went to church as usual. The sermon was about forgiveness and making things right. Carol's silent tears stained the seat cushions. Keith put his arm around her and held her close to him.

After church, she didn't eat lunch, but retreated to her room once again. She knelt next to the bed and heaved out a tired prayer.

"God, I thought I had put this all behind me. It's been festering like an abscess inside of me all this time. Lord, let me let go and truly forgive. I can't do it on my own."

She somehow summoned the strength to stretch out on top of the covers once more, and her shoes fell to the floor with gentle thuds. Again, she dreamed of pieces of the past.

She was thirteen when Ralph moved into the house. Her Daddy's life insurance had paid off the mortgage, and—she bitterly deduced—that was why her mother could feel secure dating a man with a part-time job.

The refrigerator, which was always empty after Mitch's death, was always full of fruit, meats, vegetables, milk, and juice. Her Mom, rather than looking tired, worried, and sick, started to look younger and more relaxed. At least Mom got what she wanted. Maybe even what she needed.

Carol rolled over and grunted in her sleep.

The house had already started to fall apart by the time Ralph moved in. Her dad's vegetable garden had become wild and overgrown. Weeds had sprung up and pressed the boundaries, and she and her Mom had cut the grass around the garden but had never quite brought themselves to tear down the fencing, cut the weeds, and plant grass. Would it have been that hard? And yet, every time she'd reached for the old scythe and grabbed her gloves, Carol had always felt a familiar lump swell in her throat. Every time, she'd walked back and looked at the garden again, suddenly feeling as if it were the summer of '69 again, when she used to look at the garden and let it remind her that her dad would come home and grow vegetables with her once more.

It had turned out that Ralph was very handy around the house. After moving in, he'd gradually repaired everything—the plumbing, the roof, and the electrical connections. Then he'd replaced the wood on the porch where it was falling apart, painted each room, built cabinets in the kitchen, and added a deck on the back porch and a family room out back. All of those projects were things her dad had always said he'd get around to—but never did.

Kim and others had often noticed the good work Ralph did and complimented the family on it. "The house really looks nice!" "Wow, seems you've got the best family room in town. That's screened in, too, ain't it?" And Kim once said something that festered for years: "Your mom looks like she's happy."

"Waited too long... to tell her..." Carol slurred in her sleep. "Woulda... kicked him out... if I'd told her... sooner..."

When Carol woke up, she had a pounding headache. She wrapped ice cubes in a plastic bag, grabbed a towel, and laid the towel on the bed, then put the plastic bag on top of the towel, and then reclined again, her head pressing against the side of the cold plastic bag. She couldn't sleep for a while, but the cool ice felt amazing, like a sweet breeze on a smoldering hot summer's day. Keith brought her lemonade and sat with her for a moment.

"Ain't never gonna be easy," he said. "But I ain't never gonna stop loving you, either."

Carol smiled through tears and squeezed his hand. She nodded, and he nodded back.

CHAPTER 17

Healing

Time Indicator Here

ONE WEEK LATER, the pastor's sermon was once again about forgiveness.

"We need to make things right that are wrong, as much as human beings can," Reverend Bishop preached. "Now you see, two brothers had a falling out ten years ago. They never spoke again. One of them died recently, and the other brother is inconsolable. He came to me asking how he could get some peace about the situation, and it just grieved my heart, and yet I still had to tell him: we all get to thinking that we've got so much time in which we can make up. But see, sometimes, tomorrow never comes. These tomorrows we see today, they slip by—but we never get where we think we're going to end up. 'Someday,' we say to ourselves, in the quiet of our minds, in our heart of hearts, 'Someday I'll feel less offended. Someday I'll be able to think about it and not feel angry.' We tell ourselves these things, but in truth, those are just the excuses we tell ourselves; our way of saying that we don't like the fact that we're still angry. And it's not wrong to not like being angry. It's not even wrong to be angry; that's how we know that we're feeling something that's not supposed to be. So that's actually a good thing. But we need to move on it. We need to act on it. Being angry is not the last thing; it's the first thing. It's what tells us that we need to begin the process of forgiveness. That's why we have to reach out," he said, his voice beginning to crescendo, "before we feel like we're able to do it, before we feel different about it, because if we let that anger sit there, it with either fade because we have accepted something that is wrong and made it permanent or we will become bitter because unresolved anger turns to bitterness. We need to act on what the feeling tells us we need to do before it goes away because we are not promised anything other than the love of our heavenly Father, and we do not know how many more tomorrows we have left in which to forgive. So reach out today! And resist the urge to tell yourself that you can handle it with a little more time. Brothers and sisters, that is a lie born of pride! Nobody can handle forgiveness; that's why God so loved the world—"

—and the congregation began to stand up in patches, and some raised their hands and others called out, "Preach!" and "Amen!" and "Have mercy!" as they all recited the famous passage together—

"—that he gave his only begotten son, that who-so-ever! Believeth in him! Shall *not* perish! But have eternal life!!"

Carol was standing too, short of breath, bending a little bit at the waist, her arms extended toward the altar. "Jesus, help me. Lord, tell me what to do! I know it's nothing but God gonna work on my problem. Mercy. Lord, I need mercy!"

When it looked like she was about to faint, Keith gently slipped his arm under her armpits and helped her stumble out of the pew and toward the steps in front of the first pew.

"If you need to forgive someone today, ain't a matter how many years or months or days or minutes or seconds you've waited, if the Lord is pricking your spirit with this right now, then come on up," Bishop beckoned. "Come on up to the front here and the elders are gonna lay their hands on you."

Keith stood next to Carol as three elders' hands all shared space on her shoulders.

"Father God!" boomed Bishop. "Not by might, not by power, but—"

The congregation heartily responded along with him, "—but by my Spirit, saith the Lord!"

"And so," Bishop continued as the "Let it be!"'s and "Alleluia!"'s waned, "By your Spirit, Father God, by your Holy Spirit alive and in your church, and because we cannot do it for ourselves, for that surely is our fallen side trying to be more than it can—no, by your Holy Spirit, set these your servants free from anything that might prevent them from reconciling and freely and truly offering their forgiveness."

Carol and Keith held onto each other as the last hymns were sung, and then they and the kids went straight to the car and drove home. "Why aren't we staying for the breaking of bread?" asked Kalley. "Your mom has something important to do," Carol said quietly.

When they entered the house, Carol made straight for the phone and booked a flight to Darlington, South Carolina on Tuesday morning. On Monday, Carol would tell her department chair that she needed to take the rest of the week off. When Carol got off the phone after making her reservations, Keith asked, "Are you feeling better?"

"I need to go and apologize to Kim and to my stepfather. Then I need to say my last goodbyes and let him know that I forgive him in person."

Keith nodded. "I think that is the right way to handle the matter. You won't be at peace until you take care of this." Although Keith had his misgivings about taking the time and spending the money to go to Darlington, he also knew he was dealing with the fruit of a seed planted before his time. He also knew once Carol's mind was made up, nobody was going to change it. He asked to go with her, but she insisted, "I've got to do this on my own."

Intensity shimmered in Carol's eyes and confident energy lingered in her steps and in her words that day. Her mind operated at frequency that she hadn't felt for decades. That afternoon, as she scrubbed the sticky residue of a piece of apple pie off a pie plate and looked out at the backyard, she wondered if her mother might even be proud of her, too.

⊷⊷⊷ ⊶⊶⊶

Carol checked into the Microtel and only a few minutes later ordered a cab and went straight to Kim's house. She rang the doorbell and while waiting for someone to answer, she heard footsteps from the inside. When the door opened, she saw it was Mike, Kim's new husband.

"Come on in, Carol." He waved the cab away. He turned and called upstairs. "Kim, come downstairs. Look who's here!"

Kim came out of her bedroom. When she saw it was Carol, she was hesitant, unsure of what to say.

"Can we talk?" Carol asked in a humble voice.

Mike excused himself. "I'll run out and pick us up something to eat." He knew the two best friends wanted to be alone to work things out.

Carol spoke first. "I'm sorry, Kim, for what I said. I was wrong, that's just all there is to it. I hadn't forgiven Mom, and I hadn't forgiven Ralph, and I took it out on you. Please forgive me.

"The morning after we talked, Reverend Bishop's sermon opened my eyes and heart to everything. God spoke to me and I really listened, and that is why I'm here."

Kim reached out and hugged her. "I'm so glad we made up. I sure have missed you."

"Me, too. I love you."

They both cried, hugging each other.

"I just want to go straight to the hospital after dinner. I've wasted too much time as it is."

"Sure thing," Kim said. "What made you change your mind about coming?"

Carol paused. "I guess I've harbored too much hate for too long. My reaction to your call let me know I was far from healed."

"One thing about you, Carol, is whenever you realize you are wrong, you try to correct the situation."

"Keith didn't agree with how I treated you, either."

"Well, you were right to be angry about the rape. That's healthy. But when you let that anger turn into hate, that's dangerous. It's like Brother Braswell said this week: "When you hate someone, it's like drinking poison and expecting the other person to die.""

"Thanks, friend. I've always appreciated your honesty."

When Mike got back, he put his ear to the door. Suddenly he heard laughing and talking going on inside, and he let out a sigh of relief before calling, "Hey, I'm back. I picked up Chinese food. Moo goo gai pan."

"Good, just what I wanted."

"I'm starving," Carol chimed in.

"Good," Mike said. "Let's grub."

Carol heard her stomach growl. She was happy to have an appetite again and vaguely realized she hadn't eaten very much over the past few days.

After they ate, Carol turned to Kim. "Can you take me to the hospital?"

Kim grabbed a light sweater and they were off. Kim asked, "Do you want to stop and have a Sunday ice cream at the sweet shop like we did as kids before we go to the hospital?"

"Maybe on Sunday. It's Tuesday, after all. But I do want to see our old house." When they pulled up at the house, Carol didn't get out of the car; she just stared at their childhood home. Kim waited a few minutes, thinking Carol would give her a signal to drive on. Finally, Carol got up and slowly ambled up to her house, and walked around to the back, where she saw the old garden had been paved over. Ralph had made that area into a patio.

As she stared at the surface of the patio, she realized she wasn't standing far from where her mother had died a few years prior. Tears overcame her and, for a moment, there was no Ralph, but there was an emptiness where her mother should be, and where she should have sat with her mother on this patio to make things right.

She sank to her knees on the slate of the patio and cried to the sky, "Mom, I forgive you. But please forgive me! I love you! God, forgive me."

As she breathed deeply for the next few minutes, a weight seemed to lift from her shoulders. Slowly, she stopped crying and wiped her eyes.

After about thirty minutes, she wordlessly climbed back into the car with Kim.

"Are you all right?" Kim asked softly. "Didn't know what happened to you there for a while."

"I'm fine." She motioned to the road ahead of them. "Go on."

The closer they got to the hospital, the heavier Carol's heart became. The air seemed filled with trapped energy. Every sound seemed louder than usual as the car crossed town and finally parked in the visitor lot.

Carol and Kim walked into the reception area, and went to the information desk to get visitor passes.

When they reached the elevator, Carol turned to Kim. "Can you wait in the lobby?"

Kim nodded kindly without saying a word.

On the elevator, Carol bit her lip and pinched her eyes shut. When the doors opened with a *ding,* she strode to the nurses' station and asked which room was Ralph's. One of the nurses walked her down and knocked on the door.

"Come in," Ralph wheezed weakly.

Carol walked in reluctantly. As soon as Ralph saw her, he lit up. He had multiple IVs in his arms and he looked as though he'd lost over fifty pounds. His stomach was distended and his cheeks were swollen like a chipmunk. Kidney failure, thought Carol. You reap what you sow.

"Carol," he said hoarsely, "I prayed to God that he wouldn't let me leave this world without apologizing to the one person I had hurt the most. I know what I did to you is unforgivable. If you don't accept my apology, I understand because of what I did to you and put you through. I was wrong. I have become saved in the past years since your mother's death. My spirit keeps convicting me. What I did was dead wrong. As I come closer to death, that is what is bothering me the most, even more than dying itself. I just have to apologize and make this right."

Carol spoke up. "You know, Ralph, I've been praying myself. Before I went to church this past Sunday, and listened to what God was saying to me, I couldn't wait for the day you died. In fact, I was hoping that Kim would call me and tell me you were dead, but the sad thing is that the hate I had for you was causing problems for everyone I love. I don't know how long I carried that anger on my shoulders, but it didn't make me a better person. I forgive you and your actions in the past toward me. Hopefully, you can forgive me for my hatred of you." She reached out and gave him a hug and they both cried softly.

After a few minutes and tissues, they settled down and began to talk. After they talked a little while longer, Carol showed him some pictures of her family.

"Good looking family, Carol. Your mother would be so proud of you."

Carol smiled. "Thank you," she said, surprised to feel herself smiling. There was a subtle warmth, as if her mother's presence hovered there with them for a moment, and in that moment Carol felt through and through that her mother was at peace too. They said their goodbyes and Carol left her number with the attending nurse.

She had barely closed the door gently behind her and started to turn when a doctor came around the corner, walking briskly and hailing her. "Excuse me," he said quickly. "I'm Doctor Alfred Delgado. Are you a family member to Ralph Hardy?"

Carol hesitated. "Yes, I am. Well, he's actually my stepfather. My name is Carol."

"I'm his nephrologist. As you can tell, he's in critical condition. We're working really hard trying to find him a kidney. Unfortunately, there are not that many potential donors."

Carol nodded. Dr. Delgado paused, then continued.

"I know it's a long shot, but would you be willing to complete a compatibility test? If you're a match..." he said, glancing at Carol's eyes to gauge her reaction, "In any case, he's in dire need of a kidney."

"Thank you, doctor." Carol said, feeling her shoulders clenching a little. "Can I follow up with you later? I'm under a lot of pressure right now."

Dr. Delgado wrote his pager number on the back of a business card and handed it to Carol. "I will do everything I can to make whatever you choose work as smoothly as possible," he assured her. "Please page me with a number where I can reach you whenever you make up your mind."

As she took an elevator to the ground floor to find Kim, she grappled with the idea of giving Ralph a kidney. She should have been logical and calculating, she thought to herself, but she felt the answer coursing through her veins already.

At the reception lobby, Carol and Kim got directions to the transplant lab. However, when they got to the lab, there wasn't enough time to complete the test. The attending nurse gave Carol an appointment for the first thing the following morning.

When they left the hospital, they stopped by Carol's hotel, gathered her belongings, and checked out, smiling at each other the whole time. The next morning, before they went back to the hospital, Kim called her supervisor and took the day off. Next, Carol called the Davidsons in Atlanta.

For the time being, though, Carol didn't call Keith. She left a message for him at the firehouse so he'd know she was doing well, but she still struggled to find an explanation she thought he'd understand. And if she wasn't a match anyway, then debating with him would be time and energy spent in vain—Keith didn't have to know anything until Carol knew whether or not she was a feasible donor.

Later that morning, snacking on crackers and juice at the transplant lab, Carol looked at Kim, who smiled impishly. "Nobody on this planet can talk you out of this, and neither can Keith. But I hope you're ready to tell him one fine story about it."

→→=◉ ◉=←←

The lab paged Dr. Delgado, who burst into the waiting room with wide eyes. He made a beeline over to Carol and grasped her hand with both of his. "This is amazing," he effused. "And you are a wonderful person for being willing. Thank you so much!"

Before Carol could even reply, he went on to explain, "This is a two-to-three-hour procedure and you will be up and out in five to ten days." He paused. "If you agree, I'd like to admit you this evening. Time is running out. I can schedule the procedure for Friday morning. Providing everything goes well, you will go home on Tuesday."

Carol nodded. "Yes, I will be available. Friday is fine with me, Dr. Delgado. I just have one request." Dr. Delgado's eyebrows perked up. "Anything I can do!" he replied.

Carol smiled gently. "Don't tell Ralph who the donor is until after the surgery."

"Fine with me." Dr. Delgado beamed. "That is the best surprise present I've ever heard of."

Carol heaved a deep sigh. The real work, now, was to break the news to Keith. She knew she had to do this before she even called her job to get another week off.

Finally, she picked up a phone in the lobby and called Keith. "Keith, I have something important I have to tell you."

"What is it, baby? When will you be home?"

"Wait a minute. I've got to tell you something first. I saw Ralph and he asked for my forgiveness. And I forgave him. He's very ill because he needs a kidney transplant, but there aren't any matches in the donor registry."

"And..." Keith sounded irritated.

"And I took a blood test and I am a match."

"What?!" Carol drew the receiver away from her ear. "I don't agree with this, Carol. This is worse than when you took a chance and got pregnant with Lisa without my knowledge. No, I do not agree."

Carol said nothing. Within seconds, Keith chuckled faintly. "Wait until I get there before you make a decision, okay?"

"You'd just be wasting a trip. The surgery is in the morning."

Keith sighed. "Carol, I love you. But you keep scaring me, taking your life in your hands like you do!"

Carol waited a moment and appreciated what Keith had said. Then she whispered, "Through the whole time we were getting married, I was wishing I had made up with my mother and she was there. You know when my mother died, I never properly mourned and that's why I never really got over her death. This is how I'm going to forgive myself for how I behaved when she died. It'll also let her know that she can rest in peace."

"Well," Keith conceded, "Ain't nobody but God gonna stop you."

"I miss you, the kids, and school; don't get me wrong," she said tenderly. "And I love that you want to be here with me. Waiting for you to arrive, though, that would only delay the surgery. And it doesn't actually make it safer or easier."

Keith shook his head wistfully. "Okay, babe. Promise to call me before you go into surgery and as soon as you gain consciousness. I want to make sure you're staying good at cheating the Reaper."

"I promise," Carol said. "And I want to thank you now, but I'll thank you after the surgery."

"For what?" Keith asked, suddenly intrigued.

"I love you, Keith. You do support me, through everything, completely. I could never have done any of this without your love."

Keith actually sounded choked up. He managed to get out, "I love you, Carol. Call soon."

CHAPTER 18

The Operation

Time Indicator Here

THE SURGERY WENT according to plan. The last thing Carol remembered was lying on the operating table, counting backwards from one hundred. Before she could make it to ninety, the anesthesia had taken effect. The next thing she knew, she was waking up in Recovery with Dr. Delgado standing at her bedside.

"The surgery was a success," Dr. Delgado told her, beaming again. "You came through it with flying colors, and Ralph is in stable condition. His body is adjusting to the kidney well thus far."

When Carol made it back to her room, Kim and Mike were there waiting with a bouquet of roses. They talked for a few minutes before Carol drifted off to sleep.

When she woke up, the anesthetic clearly voided from her suddenly throbbing body, Carol picked up the phone by her hospital bed and called Keith. "The kidney transplant was a success," she said. "I'm still a little groggy, but I'm okay. I love you honey, and our girls. Kiss them for me. I'll be coming home the first of the week."

"Are you sure you're okay to travel?" Keith sounded worried.

"I'm fine, darling," she said simply. "God is greater than all of this."

"Praise God! You know Kim called and told me when you first came out of surgery. The kids and I can't wait until you get back home. We really miss you."

"Miss you, too. Love you."

"Love you more."

After she hung up, she turned to Kim and Mike. "Could you get me a wheelchair and take me to see Ralph?"

"Sure," Mike said.

When they reached Ralph's room, he was just coming to. Seeing Carol in the wheelchair, he looked alarmed. "What happened to you?"

"I needed to have a procedure done, and the time just turned out to be right, so I had it done."

Ralph looked puzzled for a moment, and then looked from his back to Carol's face. "You? You were my donor?" Carol nodded gently.

He lifted his head weakly, trying to stay awake. "I love you," he mouthed as he drifted off. "Owe you… my life."

⇥▬◉ ◉▬⇤

The day before Carol's anticipated discharge, Dr. Delgado visited her room. "Carol, you are doing well," he said. "Your blood work looks good. Your body has adjusted without any complications."

"That's good to know," she replied with a smile. "I feel great."

"However," Dr. Delgado continued, "Ralph needs additional time to get his temperature down."

"How long do you think he'll have to stay?"

"Just a couple of more days." Dr. Delgado's eyes. "We're also concerned about him staying at home alone after his release. Do you know who his primary caregiver will be for his first two at home?"

"No, I hadn't really thought of it," she said. After a moment, she continued. "I'll take care of him."

"We'll have some care acknowledgements for you and him to sign before his discharge," Dr. Delgado said. "And I have to say, he's very lucky to have you."

Carol wasted no time after Dr. Delgado left. She called home, and the nanny took a message for Keith. She called Kim and told her the news. That evening, after she completed the discharge procedure, Carol padded up to Ralph's room and fell asleep in the guest chair with a spare pillow from the closet.

After Ralph's final checkup and discharge, Kim drove Carol and Ralph to the house. "Okay, pack what you need," she said to him as she opened the car door.

As Carol turned the familiar knob on the old door. A chill ran over her arms, and for a moment she froze.

Ralph watched Carol from a few steps away. After a long pause, he said, "You know, you don't have to take care of me if you don't want to."

Carol's eyes were filled with tears, yet she refused to let a tear fall from her eyes. She pushed the door open and gestured. "Get your things."

Ralph nodded. He went into the house, and Carol prayed for strength and forgiveness. Unsure of what it even meant or even how to do it, she prayed over the past. She called for love to quell her fear. "God, I am doing this for the righteousness of You," she whispered. With that, Carol squared her shoulders and went into the house.

⊸▣ ▣⊷

When Carol and Ralph arrived at Bradley International Airport, Keith and the girls met Carol with open arms. Keith was cordial to Ralph. Keith had stowed the children's clothes and toys in the original nursery and made it ready.

That became Ralph's room, and over the next few days they found he fit into their home without being obtrusive. He made sure he wasn't a burden and he helped out whenever and however he could. They fit him into their schedule of work, going to church, and running errands. He took care of the children while they cooked, and helped read to them at night in the family room. Carol never let him put the girls to bed, but it didn't feel like something he wanted to do, either. The girls grew attached to him, and were sad when it was time for him to go back to Darlington.

The two weeks flew. Kalley, who was a much more outgoing than Lisa, and had really taken to Ralph. She cried when he said he had to go down South.

Carol took a photo with her Instamatic camera. Ralph wrote his phone number on the back. "Here, baby girl," Ralph said, handing it to Kalley. "My picture and my phone number. I'm always just a phone call away."

Carol wrote Ralph a welcome home note quickly after everyone else had gone to bed. In the morning, she slipped it into the outgoing mail slot.

Part Two

CHAPTER 19

Kalley and Lisa

Time Indicator Here

AS THE YEARS passed, the two sisters grew. Always the fashionista, Kalley wanted to keep up with the Joneses and have the latest clothes and accessories—and she always had to be the center of attention. Her schoolwork was just good enough to keep her parents off her back. Whenever there was a party or sports event, she had to be there. She tolerated Lisa and sometimes treated her kindly, but only when it gave Kalley what she wanted. When they were small, they had been close. In fact, they had been inseparable. But once Kalley became a teenager, she didn't think Lisa was popular enough to hang out with.

Lisa, on the other hand, was content to wear whatever her mother bought her as long as it matched and was clean. She also didn't mind getting hand-me-downs from Kalley, nor did she complain when Kalley got new clothes. As far as grades were concerned, Lisa stayed on the honor roll. Within the family, she kept to herself and harbored her own thoughts quietly. She tried to stay close with Kalley for several years, but eventually she realized Kalley tended to use her, and Lisa allowed Kalley more distance. That was fine with Kalley, too; when Kalley's friends were around, she didn't want to be bothered with Lisa at all.

→➤◉ ◉◄←

The summer before Kalley started high school, Kim called and asked Carol, "Can the girls come for the summer to spend time with their godmother?"

"That would be wonderful!" Carol exclaimed. Over the years, the girls had always traveled with them to visit their grandparents in Atlanta, but she had never let them stay for the summer. But after years as a full-time working mother, she was getting tired, and she could use a break.

When Kim asked Kalley, she was excited. "Oh, yes, I'd love to go to Aunt Kim's!" However, Lisa declined. "No, thank you." Later, Carol told Kim, "Lisa's always afraid she'll get sick away from home. She's never been as strong as Kalley. Don't take it personal."

"She never wants to leave home," Kalley teased at the dinner table that night. "She just likes to be with her momma and daddy, the big baby."

Keith glanced at her sternly. "Stop bothering your sister." Kalley stopped, but behind her father's back, she stuck out her tongue at Lisa.

Kim agreed to pick Kalley up the week after school let out. Kalley was packed and ready to go when Kim and Mike pulled into their driveway. She ran out and greeted them both.

Carol and Keith came out and met them at the door. "Got dinner ready and we can relax and catch up on old times," Carol said and hugged her friend.

"Have you gained a few pounds?" Kim asked as she kissed Carol on the cheek. "Keith must be feeding you really well."

They both laughed as Carol reminded her she looked like she was not missing any meals either.

Kim looked at the girls with fresh eyes since she hadn't seen them in two years. They both were beginning to bloom, but Kalley was far more defined and mature-looking.

"The girls have really grown up!" she said, shaking her head and smiling. "Can't believe how big you both are. We have some fun things planned for you for the summer. Lisa, are you sure you don't want to come? There is swimming at The Y, and there's amazing stuff at summer camp. Also, a new mall just opened close to the house. It's the new teen hangout. You'll really enjoy that. Lots of new families in the neighborhood; girls your age in almost every house."

Lisa finished a bite of asparagus unhurriedly. "Maybe next time."

The next morning, Kim, Mike, and Kalley hit the road.

After two weeks in South Carolina, Kalley called her Mom. "Mom, I'm ready to come home."

"No, honey," Carol said, smiling a little bit as she remembered her first semester away from home. "You will be there for the summer so make the best of it. Your Dad and I are going to drive halfway to meet and bring you home at the end of summer."

"Okay," Kalley relented. She was missing home, her friends, and even though she hated to admit it, she missed Lisa.

-->==◎ ◎==<--

One night at bedtime, Kim brushed Kalley's hair.

"What were my parents like when they were young?" Kalley asked. She had to make conversation or do something—anything, really—to make the South Carolina summer speed up. And it would have been easier if there were some boys around.

Kim put the brush down and smiled. She sat on the bed next to Kalley. Her eyes gleamed as her thoughts walked down memory lane.

"When your parents were newlyweds, they laughed a lot. They both worked hard at the same jobs they have now. When your mom found out she was pregnant, your dad surprised her and bought the house so the baby could come home to his own home."

"'His' home?" Kalley asked skeptically.

"The doctor thought the baby was a boy, at first. But your mom and dad were just as happy to have a healthy little girl."

Kalley took a few seconds to digest the idea. Then she asked, "Did Mom like the house?"

"Of course. She loved it. Your dad painted your room, decorated it, and put the crib up. When your Mom came home, all she had to do was sit down. Your Dad did everything for her. They were both so excited about you!"

She smiled. "Yeah... maybe that's why I love my room so much."

"After you were born, your mom wanted to have a boy for your dad. Your mom decided to try and have a baby against the doctor's advice—well, against everyone's advice, really. We were all scared to death because she could have died. You know how stubborn the women in your family can be?"

"Yeah."

"When she got pregnant with Lisa, your parents both hoped it was a baby boy."

"I wish she had been a boy. We don't get along. Not like sisters should."

"You will. Siblings always disagree when they are growing up. It's known as sibling rivalry. However, when you're grown, you will be each other's best friends."

"I don't think so," Kalley said.

Kim continued the story. "Anyhow, toward the end of the pregnancy, your Mom got so sick they both almost died."

"Mom never told me that."

"Did you ever ask?"

"No, I guess I didn't."

"Well, your Mom had two high-risk pregnancies. She had a hard time with you; you came early and she had to have an emergency C-Section. Then your mom knowingly risked her life to have Lisa. She was born three months premature, and needed to stay in the hospital a long time after your mom came home. It's taken Lisa a long time to physically get strong and catch up. Guess that's why she's always been more studious. Spends more quiet time reading, studying, and learning."

They both paused, and the sound of the brush pulling through Kalley's hair blended with the muted buzzing of cicadas in the trees.

"But know one thing," Kim said heartily. "You both were conceived in love, and your parents only want the best for you. They love their two girls."

About three weeks before school would resume, Kim and Mike met Carol and Keith in Washington, D.C., a good halfway point between Darlington and New Haven. After a meal together, both families got back on the highway and headed home in opposite directions.

Chapter 20

Sibling Rivalry

Time Indicator Here

KALLEY AND TWO of her best friends, Betty and Chelsea, sat on the floor in her bedroom two days after Kalley's return from South Carolina. Her friends were acting like Kalley was a celebrity who'd returned from a world tour, and Kalley played the role to the hilt. Betty, who lived next door, was friends with both Kalley and Lisa. She spent more time with Kalley because they were the same age and in the same grade.

Lisa, who had been studying in her bedroom, went to the kitchen and made herself a snack. As she passed Kalley's room, she overheard the girls discussing high school concerns. Lisa slowed a little, trying to hear some more of the conversation.

Kalley suddenly turned to Lisa. "Did I tell you that you could come in my room?"

"No, but you didn't have to," Lisa snapped. "The door was open."

"Yes, I do, so get out."

Lisa retorted, "I will when I am finished talking."

They went back and forth arguing until Lisa threw her hand up in a "forget you" sign, and retreated down the hallway.

As Lisa receded down the hall, Kalley called after her, "You don't belong in my room—or in this house!"

Lisa replied, "Yeah, right!" and kept walking. She had already disappeared into her room when Kalley added, "Mom and Dad wanted a boy, not you. Your room was really decorated for a boy."

Betty and Chelsea were horrified. "Why you gotta go saying something like that to her?" Betty asked. Chelsea was more aggressive, pulling Kalley back down by the pant leg and scolding her. "Don't go in on your little sister like that, girl. Chill!"

Lisa had heard, though. Maybe that explained why Kalley's room was pink and hers was light green. Without the white trimming and cornice board with baby doll prints, it could have been decorated for a boy or a girl.

She also thought about the brand new boy-themed toys she found in a chest in the basement. Mom said they were there if they ever had a little boy in the future. Lisa also thought about the fact that Kalley got more attention than she did, even from Kim.

Lisa shrugged after a minute of silent thought. Then she took out her journal and her favorite pen. As she opened to a new page, she whispered, "You were supposed to be a boy, too, then."

→▬ ◯ ▬←

The next day Keith and Kalley went to Hamden High School for registration. Carol and Lisa stayed home and straightened up the house.

"Are you glad your sister is back?" Carol asked absentmindedly. Then she chided herself inside; everyone in the family already knew the answer to that question.

A pause, then Lisa stopped dusting the mantle and turned to face Carol. "No," she said in a lower register than usual. "I wish she would have stayed gone. I hate her."

Carol was shocked, and remained quiet for a moment. She'd known Lisa didn't like Kalley, but she'd underestimated Lisa's animosity.

She measured her words. "Hate is a strong word that too many people throw around lightly. Do you really mean it, to the dictionary definition?"

"Loathe, despise, repudiate, abhor—how do you want me to say it?" she asked tersely. "You see who she is. You see who I am. Even if you don't understand, I have my reasons."

"Far be it from me to tell you that you can't do anything," Carol said wisely. "Because I'm about to do something your father and I promised we would never do."

Lisa couldn't completely hide the curiosity. She watched and listened carefully.

"For me to tell you, you must promise me two things: one, that you can never tell anyone, even your sister; two, that if this story means anything to you, you will look past the mean and wrong things that your sister says or does and be there for her. Someday, although we pray not soon, your father and I won't be there. When that time comes, you'll be all each other has."

Lisa gave a tiny nod without breaking eye contact. "I promise," she said solemnly.

"You need to know the word 'hate' is a powerful word, and I say that because I know what it really means. Until I married your father, I held a lot of hate inside me for many years. I hated one person in particular, and I resented another one almost as much. But eventually, as he always does, God got my attention. The person who raped me trashed my relationship with my mom. I hated him so badly that I wished death on him every day for decades. But after God got through to me, I forgave him and risked my life to save his. It was not easy, and I don't want you to think I'm trying to tell you this so that you'll know what a wonderful person I am. Please understand: I'm telling you this story because it's what life requires and what God wants. You can tell yourself that you'll do what you want, but no person stands alone, ever. You're connected to the people you hate; you couldn't really hate them if you hadn't gotten so close. You and your sister are blood, and you two will be bonded forever, no matter what she does and no matter what you do. Don't be like I was, spending more than twenty years dying quietly because of the hatred I held inside. Please don't think that it won't affect you, because it will—whether you like it or want it or realize it or not."

Carol's eyes welled up, and Lisa felt an urge to hug her mother. She hung back, though, thinking deeply about what Carol had said but maintaining a placid face. She raged against the idea of forgiving Kalley.

⇥►⬧◉ ◉⬧◄⇤

In early October, Keith's father was in a bad car accident. Carol, Keith, and the girls headed south immediately. They flew out the morning after Kevin's accident, with Keith worrying the whole way. They all knew Kevin was in critical condition and the doctors hadn't held out much hope. Keith had spent the afternoon scrambling, trying desperately to get the first flight with four tickets available. When they arrived at the hospital, though, Kevin had already passed.

Keith's brother greeted him in the hallway, slowly embracing Keith and saying, "Pops went out fighting. Anyone else would have died at the scene of the accident."

The brothers scrambled to plan for their mother and teenage sister, Leigh. The two women living in the big house just seemed like too much. Eventually, they sat down and asked Gwen and Leigh if they'd move in with one of the brothers' families.

"No," Gwen said with a smile. "I know you all love us very much. I know Kevin won't be there anymore, but I love our home, too, and I'm going to stay here." She looked around the circle at the boys' faces. "I will be fine here. Leigh will be going off to college soon, and she needs a place to come home to, just like you boys had."

The brothers looked from one to the next, slowly, and then nodded quietly. "We're going to be calling, Mom," Keith said. "And we're going to be visiting," the others assured her.

CHAPTER 21

Kalley, Lisa, and Betty

Time Indicator Here

LISA STARTED AT Hamden as a freshmen in the fall, and anyone who didn't know her last name wouldn't have known that she and Kalley were related. As always, Lisa was all about her work. She only had a few friends, one of whom was Betty. She was very close with her friends; even more so because Lisa wasn't really into boys.

Predictably, Kalley was into everything about school except her work. She was always at the center of a loud, laughing bunch of students in the classroom, hallway, cafeteria, or parking lot.

Betty and Kalley had been friends since elementary school, but they got even closer when Betty's family moved into the house next door. Betty and Kalley were frequent guests at each others' houses, allegedly so they could do homework and study together.

Betty dated Eric Holden, a freshman starter on the Varsity basketball team. Lisa was aware of that, as was the whole school—everyone saw them kissing in the hallway. Lately, though, Eric had been calling the house asking for Kalley more than once a week.

Lisa asked her sister, "Why is he always calling you?"

Kalley tossed her hair and her large hoop earrings jiggled. "I'm helping him with a homework assignment," she said flippantly. *Whatever,* Lisa thought. *Maybe he's trying to hook Kalley up with one of his boys.*

One afternoon, Lisa looked for her history notebook but couldn't find it. Then she remembered: Betty had taken it home to copy notes from the day before. She walked to the upstairs phone, picked it up, and almost started to dial.

But she heard Eric's voice first. "When we meet this time, come back over to my house."

Then Kalley asked, "Where's Betty going to be?"

"Studying with Lisa, as usual," he said with a chuckle. Kalley laughed too. Lisa hung up the phone gently.

Lisa went downstairs and poured herself a lemonade from the fridge, which was right next to the downstairs phone. "What are you doing?" she asked Kalley. "You barely do your own assignments! What kind of help could you really give Eric? And Betty's the better student, anyway. Why doesn't he study with her?"

"None of your business," Kalley replied snippily.

"So Betty is your friend, but you're sneaking around with Eric? You know you're playing with fire, right?"

Kalley shot Lisa a stern look and repeated, more slowly and ominously, "Mind. Your own. Business."

"It's wrong to take her man, Kalley. I know you're God's gift to all men everywhere, all at the same time, but it's still wrong." Kalley genuinely seemed stunned at Lisa's boldness. Before she could say anything, Lisa went on. "You should come clean to Betty."

Kalley, arms akimbo, spoke with syrupy condescension. "I know this is hard for you to understand, because you're perfect score Lisa in every subject except anatomy, but I'll say it real slow for you: miiind your ooooooown bizzzness."

"Well, she's my friend, too, and I'm going to do what I would want her to do if she caught you running around with my boyfriend. If you really are helping him with homework, then you shouldn't have a problem with telling her—or with me telling her, either."

"I'm not telling her nothing. I'm not going out with her, he is." Kalley looked at Lisa defiantly.

"Well, I'm sure she'll be happy to know that you're not going out with her," Lisa said, walking upstairs with a certain lilt in her step.

It took about twenty-four hours for Kalley to feel the heat. Betty listened quietly as Lisa told her about her sister seeing Eric on the sly. She called Eric right away, but the call went to voicemail. Betty didn't say anything, but she stormed out of the house.

Later, when Kalley was walking home past Betty's house, Betty invited Kalley to stop for an iced tea.

"Nah, but thanks!" she replied cheerily without breaking stride. "I gotta—"

"Gotta what?" Betty interrupted. "Gotta go help someone with the homework? With the homework you don't write down or understand or do? Girl, I gave you credit and faith. I thought what everyone else said was just jealousy because they don't have the bodies to keep up with us. But girl, don't act like you couldn't get your own boy toy. That's bad. And don't lie to me about doing your homework. That's worse. And don't forget that we are no longer friends. That's the biggest mistake."

Kalley couldn't say anything. Speechless with rage, she ran home to confront Lisa.

"Lisa!" she bellowed, charging up the stairs. "How could you put my business out there for everyone? I hope you like the mess you made!"

"So you really thought you could just sleep with your friend's boyfriend? And that you wouldn't get caught?"

"You should have minded your own business!!" Kalley howled as she stomped into her room and slammed the door.

Lisa followed her and stood outside her door. "You were going to wait for her to find out so that she could ask me whether or not I was holding out on her? And then what? Then you would have destroyed two relationships. I stopped you after you destroyed one. I'm involved, so it is my business. It always has been."

The argument carried over into school. Betty and Kalley got into an altercation in the hallway after their first period class. Their parents met the principal for a debrief that marked the start of their first suspensions.

Betty told Eric to stay with Kalley. Kalley and Betty didn't speak at all. Of course, Betty and Lisa became closer than ever, and they both studied together and dominated the honor roll.

CHAPTER 22

Sunday

Time Indicator Here

"KALLEY, ARE YOU ready for church?" Carol asked through the closed bedroom door.

"Mommy, the cramps are bad this morning, really bad. I'm just going to take some aspirin and try to get some sleep."

"You didn't go to church last Sunday. Seems like this is becoming a habit, young lady," Carol said, opening the door.

"It's not my fault, Mommy. This week my body isn't giving me a break. Last week I needed to study for my exam on Monday morning. I've got to keep my grades up!"

"You have not gone to church all month, young lady."

"The week before I couldn't get my hair done, and you know I can't go if I'm not looking good."

"Honey, you've got a lot to learn about life. The first to go will be your looks. Don't base your life on that. You will be sorely disappointed." Shaking her head and turning, she looked at Keith, who was straightening his tie as he walked toward the stairs.

"Keith, talk to your daughter."

"Carol, what can I say to that?" *If she were my son*, he thought, *I'd tell him to move his butt.* "Honey?" he called, but Carol had already walked down the hall.

Keith looked at his watch. "We're leaving here in ten minutes. Everybody going can meet me in the car. We're not going to be late."

"Lisa, are you ready?"

"Yes, Mom. I'll be right down."

Lisa walked into Kalley's room.

Kalley looked up from her bed. "Who told you you could come in my room? I didn't hear you knock," she sneered.

"Come kick my—oh, wait. You have cramps. I almost forgot. And all I wanted was to borrow your blue cardigan," Lisa sighed half-mockingly.

"No."

The blue cardigan was draped over the closet doorknob.

"Why? I just want to wear it to church. I'll take good care of it."

"No," she repeated. "Get out of my room."

Lisa looked at the cardigan and took a step toward the closet, but then stopped, turned, and walked back into the hall.

"Kalley, don't talk to your sister like that," Carol said as she passed in the hallway. "That's the only sister you have."

"Thank goodness for that," Kalley stage whispered.

"Lisa always lets you borrow her things. Now you be a nice, young lady, and lend the sweater to your sister. You do not pay for the clothes or the bills around here, Missy."

"Mom, that's not fair." Kalley pulled the covers over her head and rolled back over in the bed.

Keith was already in the car, honking the horn. Carol and Lisa hustled out to the driveway and in moments, the car was gone. Kalley watched through the sheer curtains in her window. Then walked to the phone and dialed Richard's number.

Kalley had met Richard during her junior year. He was a junior at Hillhouse High at the time. They'd met downtown, where most high school teens hung out after big sporting events. Richard transferred to Hamden after Hillhouse expelled him.

Richard was always immaculately dressed. He was a sneaker head, but not a pure collector. He proudly sported a new pair almost every day. It was hard to tell, because his collection was so big that even if he wore a different pair every day it would take months to get back to the first pair. He also had his own car, a Honda Civic with shiny rims and a giant subwoofer system. You could always tell Richard was driving through the area because the bass shook the car and everything nearby. He was always accompanied by a short boy, an eighth grader everyone called Little Red.

Keith and Carol only spoken with Richard twice—and only in passing—when he dropped Kalley off or picked her up. Keith tried to learn more about Richard from Kalley. "What does he do? Does he work?"

Carol was curious about different things. "Why does he always have that little kid with him? Who are his parents? When are we going to meet them?"

Kalley was evasive and reminded her parents that this was high school. She hinted that Richard would be temporary. For a little while, Keith and Carol waited to see if that would turn out to be the case.

Richard was always in the background, but signs of Richard's generosity were obvious. Kalley would shamelessly debut his gifts, such as a gold necklace with a matching bracelet, at school. Sometimes she'd take them off at home, but sometimes she'd forget. She wore her new three-hundred dollar True Religion jeans and a new pair of limited edition Michael Jordan sneakers to the dinner table one night. Everyone noticed, but nobody said anything. The longer that went on, the smugger Kalley got.

"Hey, baby," she half-whispered into the phone. "They're gone. You coming over this morning? I need a repeat performance like last Sunday, you know."

She blushed as she thought of all that went on in her bedroom last Sunday.

"Yeah, babydoll, I'll be right there," he replied softly.

"We just have two hours. I'll keep it hot for you 'til you get here," Kalley crooned as she hung up the phone.

"I'm on my way."

Richard didn't care that they were on a schedule; being with Kalley was like having a college girl.

When the doorbell rang, Kalley flew, feet barely touching the floor, and flung open the door. She pulled Richard in and closed the door quickly. She checked outside through the front window, hoping the neighborhood watch neighbor, Mrs. Griffin, was not home. Usually she was at church, and when Kalley saw no lights or motion in her house, she smiled and spun around to face Richard.

"One hour and twenty-five minutes. Then you'll have to be out the door," she reminded him between kisses.

"I missed you, baby," he said, pulling her close and then letting her go.

"What you got for Daddy?" He teased as he ran his hand in between her legs. She moaned in anticipation, grabbed his hand, and led him upstairs. "Baby, Daddy's gonna take care of you."

They slipped into the bed, caressing each other hungrily. "Did you put a rubber on?" she whispered.

"Oh, yeah. Daddy's taking good care of you."

⇥⟡ ⟡⇤

As Keith drove them to church, Lisa asked her mom, "Why does she act like that?"

"Like what?" her mom asked.

"Kalley always borrows my clothes without asking. And she never knocks on my door; she just comes in. What hurts the most, though, is that she'll say and do anything until she gets what she wants. I know I shouldn't fall for it every time, but every time she starts saying that we need to be closer and she's sorry about what she's done, I keep hoping maybe she means it and fantasizing about what it would be like if we were friends as well as sisters."

After a short silence, Lisa half-coughed. "Never mind. I knew I was just being weak and gullible before I even asked. I shouldn't have said anything."

Carol tried to smooth it over. "She's just not as mature as you are, even though she's older."

"Are you sure we are sisters? She acts like I'm not related to her. We don't look alike. No one even knows we are sisters unless I tell them. And in public, if it does come out that we're related, she acts all ashamed."

"She has always wanted to be the center of attention, even when she was a very little girl," Keith remarked. "I can't figure out exactly why she still pushes it so hard—sometimes I think it's because she didn't get the attention that she wanted, but other times I think it's because she got exactly what she wanted."

Keith hit the turn signal and made the next turn. "Can't really decide what's truer, though," he added under his breath.

Carol forced a smile as she scanned the rearview mirror for Lisa's face. "I'm sure eventually she will mature and treat you more lovingly."

When they arrived at church, Carol and Keith went to the sanctuary. Lisa warmed up with the rest of the choir downstairs.

As Lisa approached the doors to the warm-up area, Betty came out.

"What's up, Leese?" she said, her face a giant, radiant smile.

"Hey, girl," Lisa said, flashing an "I-can-recover" half-grin.

Betty added everything up quickly. "Come on—I gotta freshen up. Walk with me." Lisa fell into step with her. "Wait—where's Kalley? Upstairs?"

"At home," Lisa scowled. "She was crampy."

Betty smiled.

"I don't think it's that funny," Lisa fumed. She waited until the restroom door closed behind them and then scanned the stalls for shoes. When she saw none, she scoffed. "My personal pain in the ass has a pain in the ass, so she stays home."

Betty's grin tempered with compassion as she reached into her clutch and took out a compact. "Her cramps would only hurt their worst on a Sunday morning, you know."

"What do you mean? She gets crampy whenever she can." Lisa leaned on the counter and watched the reflection of Betty doing her makeup in the mirror on the opposite wall.

"Well," Betty said in between eyeliner strokes, "Kalley's thinking that she's mending our broken friendship. Now you and the rest of the world already know that I will never trust her again. But she's still trying to do the whole 'tight like sisters' thing. So she told me on Friday she wouldn't be at church."

"Did she say why?" Lisa asked, unable to hide her curiosity.

"Don't be naïve and, by all means, don't tell your parents," Betty warned.

"I have tried and tried, but I just don't understand her. Makes no sense at all. This new guy of hers, Richard, is all the news unfit to print."

Betty smudged the red across one side of her face as she spun around, dropping the lipstick and bracing Lisa's shoulders in one swift move. "Hold the bus a sec, girl," she exclaimed.

Lisa tried to keep her composure, but started to chortle. "Hold the bus hostage, maybe, Joker?" she asked, turning Betty around toward the near mirror. The two girls collapsed into laughter, steadying themselves on the vanity as they teetered in their shiny Sunday heels.

"Let me fix this," Lisa said, still smiling, as she wet a tissue under the faucet and then wiped and dabbed Betty's smear until it was gone.

"For real, though," Betty said, forced to hold still while Lisa worked.

"For real what?" Lisa said, resisting the opportunity to rib Betty again.

"You said Richard, right?"

"Yeah…"

"Richard like Eight Ball Rich?"

A cold chill ran down Lisa's back. "Oh, shit." Lisa stopped dabbing and leaned against the vanity again. Everyone had heard of Eight Ball Rich. According to the stories, he was a twentysomething boss who ran cocaine in New Haven. Some people said he'd faked his age so he could stay in high school. Nobody ever said who he was, but everybody could name someone who worked for him.

"You're right about that," Betty said. Lisa shivered.

CHAPTER 23

Bad News

Time Indicator Here

Dear Mom and Dad,

Sometimes I've been mad at Kalley, but please understand that I'm writing you this note with her safety and nothing else in mind.

I think Richard, the guy Kalley goes out with, is a big-time drug dealer called Eight Ball Rich. I don't even know if Kalley understands or cares about how Richard gets his money and free time, but Eight Ball Rich is no small-time weed flipper.

If I tell her, she won't listen because she hates me. If you tell her, maybe she'll listen. I think if she knew how risky it was, she wouldn't be doing what she's doing. I just hope we can get her out of this situation.

Lisa

"KEITH," CAROL SAID, realizing she had tried to speak louder than she actually had. She cleared her throat quietly. "Keith, are you still downstairs?"

Keith entered from the kitchen, drying his hands on a dishtowel. "What's up, babe?"

"Did you see this?" Carol handed him the handwritten letter.

⋗⋗▬◉ ◉▬⋖⋖

By the time Lisa walked in from school, her stomach was a butterfly pavilion. Her head wished she'd never written the note, but her heart was glad she did.

She opened the door slowly. In the living room, Keith sat in the large chair, brows furrowed, his fingers tapping silently on his knee. Carol was wearing a dress Lisa had never seen before and sitting primly in the small chair like a secretary ready to take notes. Lisa tried to enter without drawing their attention, as if she were the one dating the drug dealer.

"You did the right thing," Keith said without turning. Lisa hesitated and peered into the living room. Carol had gotten up and walked toward the hallway. She wrapped Lisa in her arms and, in a voice Lisa had never heard, said calmly but coolly, "We'll get to the bottom of this." Her arms ran up and over her mother's shoulders and she sighed languidly.

⇥═◉ ◉═⇤

Richard took off the medical gloves and smiled. He put his work bag—an identical backpack to the one he used for school—next to the door. He dialed a number.

"Yeah, you ready?" He examined his outfit in the mirror: black with silver trim. "Aight, let's work. I'll get you in five." He hung up and tossed the backpack over his shoulder.

When Richard arrived at the Farnam Courts, Little Red sauntered over and hopped in. "You late," Little Red said casually. "You keeping Lorraine company?"

Richard nodded. "Yeah, sometimes."

"Sometimes? What's that mean?"

"She worked with me before you did. You know, we'd already been hitting it for a little while, had our own place and whatnot. But then she started using. You already know 'bout that."

Little Red smiled. "Don't trust no junkie."

"Yessuh," Richard sighed. "And I got my moms and my sis to look after."

"An' she always look like she want another taste," Little Red remarked. Richard nodded.

"She's clean for now," he said deflatedly. "But it's just a matter of time before she goes 'round again."

"At least she ain't gonna talk."

"What you tryin' to say?" Richard snapped. "You think Kalley gonna rat?"

"I ain't sayin' nothin' 'xcept what it is," Little Red retorted with a scowl. "Is she ride or die or not?"

"She ride," Richard said, smirking. "Don't know about the die part yet, but she kept her dad off my back."

They pulled into an alley and drove through to a small parking lot, where they got out of the car and strode toward the building. "Showtime," Little Red said, checking his pistol. Richard nodded. "Yessuh."

→—◉ ◉—←

"I do love me some Richard!" Kalley thought to herself. She forced herself to hold the smile back from her lips as she walked down the street. "Poker face," she said to herself.

Even her finest poker face wasn't ready for what was waiting for her in the living room. Keith didn't even say anything; he simply gestured to the couch. Carol spoke first.

"Kalley, we need to meet Richard."

"You both have met Richard a lot of times."

"No, we have seen him many times. We see him when he comes and pick you up. You always rush him out the door. We never get a chance to talk with him," Keith clarified slowly.

"And he's, well, different," Carol added. "We want to meet him, but that other boy is always with him too. He can't be more than twelve or thirteen."

Her Dad looked at her. "I suppose you're going to tell me that he goes and picks up this kid's girlfriend from the elementary school and that the four of you go on double dates to the library." Kalley didn't answer. "You get on that phone right now, young lady, and tell Richard your parents want to meet him in half an hour. He will come speak with us himself, and he will leave his secretary at home."

Kalley shuddered. Her father seemed calm in an odd way, but she could feel the undercurrent of quiet anger underneath it all. She reluctantly walked to the phone and called Richard.

After a few minutes, she returned to the living room. "He'll be here in a few," she said with muted indignation.

Within thirty minutes, Richard pulled up and parked in front of the house. He stepped out of his blue Honda Civic and walked slowly to the front door.

CHAPTER 24

The Dilemma of Richard

Time Indicator Here

KEITH OPENED THE front door. He immediately noticed Richard's sneakers. Keith didn't know much about sneakers, but he knew he'd never seen any sneakers even remotely like Richard's. They were purple with yellow trim, and tiny black filigree filled the side panels. He suddenly realized that Kalley had a matching pair, which she always wore with the gold chain necklace and bracelet. He looked at Richard's neck and there was a matching gold chain.

Richard scanned the living room carefully. He felt as if he were looking into a living museum. The cherry wood furniture was well kept and polished. Family pictures graced the walls. The hardwood peeked out from the edges of the colorful area rug in the center of the room.

"We haven't been formally introduced. This is my wife, Carol, and I'm Keith. Kalley has mentioned you often."

Carol extended her hand to Richard. "Glad to meet you."

Keith cut right to the chase. "So: Richard, what exactly do you do? Do you work?"

Kalley heaved a sigh and looked exasperated. "Dad," she said with a groan.

Keith looked at her. "Understand this: you are my oldest daughter. It's my job to keep you safe, from hurt, harm, and from danger." He turned back toward Richard again. "I'll ask my questions again. Richard, what do you do? And where do you work? And please know that whatever claims you make I will verify."

"I'm a hustler for any chance I can get. I bet on anything that will make money—anything except drugs. I shoot pool for money and bet on sporting events."

"Do your parents know what you do?" Keith looked straight into Richard's eyes. Richard looked directly back into Keith's eyes. "My dad died before I really understood death. But he didn't support us anyway. My mom, she's a nurse's aide at Yale New Haven, but that's not enough to pay the bills and care for me and my younger sister. Plus, she still needs to have clothes for herself and keep her car running. So my mom and I made a deal: as long as I stick with school and don't sell drugs, she doesn't ask how I make money. After all, I did all this to help her out."

Keith thought for a moment. "Richard, the problem is, I don't want my daughter around a high-risk lifestyle. She's too young and impressionable. She shouldn't be looking for a boyfriend or husband that's counting on a bet or anything in the streets to support a household or family. So, if you find a job and change your way of living it would be okay for you to continue seeing each other, but until then, you hanging out with our daughter is unacceptable."

"That's why I never sat down and talked to you. I knew you wouldn't think he was good enough for me!" Kalley screamed. She burst into tears and ran upstairs to her room.

"I understand what you're saying," Richard replied smoothly. "I'll find a job, if that's what it takes to have a relationship with your daughter. I really care for Kalley. I want the best for her as well, sir."

Richard turned around to leave, then hesitated and looked over his shoulder. "I'll be back when I find a job."

→─═◉ ◉═─←

Keith and Carol went upstairs to talk to Kalley. She locked her door and refused to talk to them.

"Kalley, open up, honey," Carol called through the door.

Kalley stayed face down on her bed. "I'm a senior," she whispered as she pulled the pillow down onto her head as hard as she could. "Eighteen. I'm grown. I love Richard and he loves me."

After a long silence, Carol looked at Keith. "Let's leave her alone," he said quietly. "We'll talk later when she's calmed down."

CHAPTER 25

The Pregnancy

Time Indicator Here

KEITH AND CAROL talked about their meeting with Richard. They didn't need to do any fact checking to be sure that Richard was dealing drugs. As if to silently confirm it, Richard kept his word and stopped coming to see Kalley. A few months later, Carol remarked on his disappearance as she served dinner to Keith and Lisa.

"I think Kalley has finally gotten over that horrible Richard."

Lisa let out a dry guffaw. "I see them all the time in school. Sometimes I think they skip classes together."

Keith shook his head in disgust. "Well, I suppose we could drop her off and pick her up from school."

"Keep Kalley on permanent lockdown?" Carol asked, eyebrows raised. "That's not practical. I'm still teaching when she gets out of school."

⸻

A few days later, the phone rang. It was Mrs. Miller, the high school principal. Keith answered the phone.

"Hello, this is Principal Miller from Hamden High. I need to speak to the parents of Kalley Davidson. I called earlier today."

"This is Keith Davidson, her father," he said proudly and assertively. "How can I help you, Ms. Miller?"

"Kalley refused to participate in gym class this morning," the principal began. "She cannot graduate without the gym credit, and her gym teacher

108

called the counseling office so that they could alert you because she has refused to participate for four classes in a row. However, I told them to wait before calling you.

"Unfortunately, I'd seen this type of behavior before and had a hunch. I talked with the nurse. I'm sorry to tell you this, but Kalley is three months pregnant. She said she would talk to both of you when she got home. Hopefully she already did that, but we are required to disclose the information."

"Well, uh, thank you very much for letting us know," Keith said slowly. "We'll follow up with you soon."

Keith hung up the phone and tried to gather his thoughts. Kalley... what were they going to do as a family? He made himself a cup of tea and sipped it slowly, pacing the kitchen slowly, before and after dinner.

Kalley arrived home late. "Dad, I need to talk to you and Mom together. It's important." Carol was grading in the living room, and Keith quietly came in and sat down next to her.

"I'm three months pregnant. The baby is due in July. Now, before you say anything, please let me finish—"

"Oh, no!" Carol sighed. "Kalley, you are so young! Why didn't you come to us first?" Carol asked.

"What about school? What about college? It's hard to raise a child. What will you do for money?" Keith tried to keep from raising his voice.

"Mom, Dad, before you get upset, please let me finish. Richard and I have already decided we want to be together and raise our kid together. So as of February first, we are moving into our own apartment."

"Kalley, we don't want you to move out because you're pregnant," both said in unison.

"We can give you all the help you need here." Carol spoke first, as she fought back tears. "Kalley, your dad and I always wanted more for you. We wanted you to finish college before you started a family. The main thing is we want you to be able to take care of yourself." She began sobbing.

Keith patted Carol's hand. "Let's handle this problem as a family."

Kalley watched her parents cry as they struggled with a blend of love and worry.

"I love you both dearly," Kalley assured them. "I appreciate your suggestion, but Richard and I have already decided what we are going to do."

"Honey, you are so young. How can you make such a major decision?" Carol asked in a gentle voice.

"I want to do what's right and raise my child with his mother and father."

"Oh, Jesus!" Carol raised her hands to the ceiling, then shook her head and took a deep breath. She explained, "It's not a formula, honey. You don't just get a place to live, put a mom and a dad in it, and expect that it makes parenting go smoothly."

"If you're worried about me finishing school, I already thought about that. I'm not due until July, so if I stay in school, I can still graduate."

Keith and Carol looked at each other briefly and thought for a moment. "What do you plan to do for money?" Keith asked.

"Do you plan to be a stay-at-home mom and count on Richard to dictate your life? And, if not, who are you going to trust to watch the baby while you are at work?"

"I'll stay at home the first year and then I'll find a job and pay for daycare on certain days. And Richard's mom said she would help out as much as she could."

Keith replied, "It's hard for me to tell you this because right now that all looks like it'll work, but you won't be able to count on Richard's hustle to keep a roof over your head and keep you fed. And I don't want to judge someone I don't know, but Richard's mom depends on him, not the other way around. If he can't provide for you, he can't provide for her either."

"Dad, I don't want to talk about it anymore. You are trying to change my mind, like Richard and I expected you would, and it's not going to work."

Kalley got up and headed to her room. She put her hand protectively over her belly.

When she left the room, Carol shook her head and turned to Keith with a pleading look. "Life has changed, but she hasn't. She's still our little girl."

Keith's shoulders slumped. "Time has gone by. She's legally grown, eighteen and free to choose."

Carol put her forearms across her thighs and cradled her face in her hands. "She still runs to her room for comfort if life gets too tough. How's she going to raise a baby?"

Suddenly the key turned in the front door. They both turned to see Lisa.

"Hi, Dad. Hey, Mom. You're up late."

"Yeah," Carol said. "We are. You, too, I guess."

"Big test tomorrow," Lisa replied. "Betty and I promised each other we'd get at least six hours of sleep, though."

Keith and Carol smiled. "You're gonna destroy it," Keith said. "Just like your mom, you got a specially-good brain." Lisa smiled and headed upstairs.

Keith and Carol retreated to their room to get ready for bed but kept discussing the situation in whispers.

"I don't know, Carol, we might have to sit back and let her fall. She's stubborn just like you. Once she makes up her mind, that's it, and she doesn't want to hear anything else."

Lisa, lying in her bed, could hear from the tones of the conversation that something serious was going on. She crept out of bed and opened her closet door stealthily. She slowly entered the closet, making her way to the wall it shared with her parents' bedroom. She pressed her ear to the wall.

"As parents, how can we let her go down a wrong road that she can't see? Isn't that as bad as giving up on our child?"

Keith sat on the edge of the bed and dropped his head in his hands. "I blame myself," he said emptily. "That was me who told Richard he couldn't see her unless he gave up the hustler's life. Maybe she wouldn't have ended up pregnant a month later."

"How could that be your fault?" Carol asked genuinely. "We were only doing what we thought was right at the time. We have to solve what's going on now. Do you think we need to talk to Richard's mom and see if she can talk them out of it?"

Keith looked at Carol in disbelief. "What good will it do to talk to a single parent who allowed her son to hustle to support her? Is she really going to tell him to straighten out? What's she gonna do in the meantime to make ends meet?"

"Keith, you're judging her. We were blessed to find each other in college and to wait until we graduated to move in together. And we've had the privilege of raising our kids together. There were times when the girls were young, when it was really challenging. And you were always supportive. I can't imagine trying to do it myself with no help."

Keith sighed. "You're right. It's not easy being a single parent, and I'm not wishing that on Kalley. What did you have in mind?"

"I remember how much my mom used to stress before she remarried."

"Okay," he said. "Tell me more."

"I'd rather have her see that she can rely on us and learn to rely on us, rather than learning to rely on Richard."

"We both know where that's going to lead."

Carol nodded. "If we support her with her move, we can expect certain things to go our way. If we pay her deposit and her first six to eight months' rent, she can stay at home to bond with the baby and search for school and work without being under even more pressure."

Keith thought about it, then got up and put on his pajamas. "I'm sure I can pick up a little used car for her. There's always someone at work selling something in fairly good shape. I'll check the message board tomorrow."

"After she has the baby, she can get herself a job in the morning, then be at home for a little while to care for the baby, and then she can go to night school. On your days off you can take care of the baby and I'll keep it at night when she has classes. If we are busy we can hire a babysitter a couple of days a week."

"If we do all that," Keith replied, "Richard would be living there for free and coming in and out as he pleases."

Carol answered. "He's going to do that anyway and there is nothing we can do or say, but at least Kalley won't be sitting around wasting her life, waiting and counting on him. This way she'll have control of her home, herself, and her destiny. If he steps up to the plate and takes care of Kalley and his child, all the better. Kalley can save her own money and help out here and there. If not, Kalley will get tired of it. And, better still, she'll be in a position to tell him to leave because she'll be able to do it all by herself. That's what she can do with our help."

"He might not be there for other reasons, too," Keith said, "Which makes our help even more important." He took off his glasses, folded them, and placed them on his end table. "But where are we going to get the money?"

"We're going to have to use Kalley's college savings, and maybe a little of Lisa's. We can replenish Lisa's account before she graduates."

—>━● ●━<—

Lisa slammed the closet door as she charged back into her room and flung herself down on her bed. She beat her fist into her pillow furiously. Through gritted teeth, she ranted with every blow to the pillow. "Congratulations, Kalley! We're so happy that you decided to screw up your life that we're going to take Lisa's college fund buy you a place to live for free, on your own, with your drug dealer boyfriend, so you can never go to church or college or worry about what goes into being responsible or successful because you clearly aren't smart enough for that. Lisa will be okay because she does things right, and she'll understand because she's a good person!" She pounded the pillow until her protests came out one word at a time, and the punches were weaker and farther apart, and eventually she cried and then fell asleep.

—>━● ●━<—

The next day Keith and Carol visited Hamden High. They wanted written approval for Kalley to finish her last six months and graduate even though she was pregnant. After meeting with the principal, they took Kalley to lunch.

At the restaurant, they went over what they were going to do for her and what they expected in return, which was for her to get a job after about eight months and then slowly work in some night classes into her schedule.

"What about Richard?" Kalley asked.

Carol's cheeks looked as if they could burst through her skin and her eyes narrowed. "What about him? That's your boyfriend, and he can stay in your place and share your time and your food and your approval at your discretion."

Kalley bit her lip for a moment and controlled herself. "Okay, thank you." As they continued to eat and the topic changed, she found herself very surprised at how supportive her parents were being. Well, except for how they basically acted as if Richard didn't exist. She calmed her anger, though, telling herself that Richard would show everyone he was better than anyone thought.

CHAPTER 26

Lisa's Pain

Time Indicator Here

SHORTLY AFTER THEIR talk, Keith and Carol bought Kalley a used silver Mazda 626 and rented a two-bedroom apartment at Ashmun Flats, a short bus ride away from Hamden High.

For the next several months, Lisa fumed silently. "Maybe I should get pregnant," she exclaimed under her breath one day as she glowered out the bus window at the New Haven neighborhoods passing by. It was a ridiculous thing to say, of course. She preferred her celibacy, especially given some of the stories and rumors she'd heard. She shook the thought off for the time being and walked to Betty's house.

"What's happening?" she asked sunnily as Betty opened the door. "I'm back. At least for now. I promise not to be too bitter while we're together."

"No offense," Betty said quickly, "but I don't even have time to get mad with you these days. Girl, I've got a new man in my life. He's really nice." The two of them chattered excitedly for a few minutes about Clarence.

"He's cool. I met him at College Exchange orientation. He's going to school for computer science, but he already codes with a German developer called Alpha. They make photo, video, and art production software."

"I know that's right!" Lisa exclaimed, high-fiving Betty. "Let me know if he has any cute friends, okay? On second thought," she said suddenly, "Let me know after graduation. Gotta take care of business and get myself a scholarship."

"Don't be so hard on yourself!" Betty scolded gently. "You deserve to go on a date every now and again."

"It's not that," Lisa said, a mild frown returning. "My parents spent my college fund on setting Kalley up with a car and a place. They say they're gonna replace the money. But they forgot that I have an A in math, so unless they both start earning five times as much as they earn right now, it would take them seven more years to do that, even if they don't give Kalley anything else. As usual, I'm on my own."

"Hey!" Betty said, mock shock on her face. "How about me?"

Lisa smiled. "You're always there for me. Thank you. You mean the world to me." She took her books out of her backpack and paused for a moment. "I guess it's easy for me to think other people have it better than I do."

"You mean Kalley?" Betty laughed. "Karma bit her in the butt for sneaking around with him when the rest of the family was at church. As my granny use to say, 'There's no secret done in the dark that don't come out in the light.'"

⊷▭ ▭⊶

At dinner, Lisa stewed as Keith and Carol verbally reviewed the details of the arrangements they'd made for Kalley.

After listening for a few minutes, Lisa interrupted. "Richard dropped out last week."

"How do you know?" Keith asked, trying to hide his alarm.

"Betty is dating a guy who grew up in the same neighborhood. He says Richard and another dealer called Little Red are on the street all day every day."

Keith was furious. "I'm going over there right now and straighten Richard out. He's got to get out of there or fly right if he's going to stay around my daughter and grandchild."

Carol touched Keith's arm gently. Keith paused and looked at Carol, who shook her head. "That is their place, and there is a time and a place for everything. We don't want them to think we are trying to run their lives because we helped Kalley. If we handle this the wrong way, one or both of them will totally shut us out."

"Carol, when is the right time?" Keith said spitefully as he sat down. "When the drug dealers drag our pregnant daughter out because of one of Richard's drug deals has gone bad?"

Carol blew her nose into her napkin. "We just have to pray. We have to give this to God and let Him work it out." Keith reached over and touched Carol's arm.

"Forgive me, babe. I don't know what to do, and I feel like there's no way for things to end well."

"Faith," Carol whispered. She blew her nose again and looked at Keith with quiet strength. "Faith."

Lisa marveled as she took another bite of mashed potatoes. Her parents looked a little older ever since Kalley's ordeal started. Keith's hair seemed greyer than before, she thought, and as she chewed she wondered what she would do if she'd had a daughter in Kalley's situation.

The night of Kalley's high school graduation, no one was prouder than Keith and Carol. Lisa took a picture of her parents with Kalley, who had never looked happier. Kalley's graduation gown fit her tightly since she was eight months pregnant, though she wasn't showing too much, and Carol noticed that her belly had dropped a little since the week before.

Almost three weeks after graduation, Kalley called in the evening. "Mom?" she said. "Is Mom there?" Carol picked up the phone as quickly as she could. "Mom, I think my water broke."

"Are you sure?"

"Yes, I was standing in the kitchen washing dishes and it felt like I'd peed on myself."

"Have you had a bloody show?"

"No. I mean, I don't think so. What is that?"

"Don't worry about that. Is Richard there?"

"No." Kalley let out a soft moan.

"Do you think you can drive yourself to the hospital?"

"No, I'm in too much pain."

"Okay. Lisa and I will be there in a few minutes to pick you up. I'll call your Dad at work and have him meet us there. Call Doctor Martin and let him know you are on the way."

"Lisa, your sister's in labor," Carol called to the bedroom upstairs. "Hurry! We're going to pick her up."

Carol called Keith at the firehouse. When he picked up the phone, she merely said, "It's time. Meet us at the hospital."

"I'll see you in a few minutes." He replied, feeling the excitement in her voice.

When Carol and Lisa arrived at Kalley's, she was already waiting for them on the porch. Lisa grabbed her little over-night bag.

"How are you doing, Sis?" Lisa asked, reaching out to help Kalley down the stairs.

"I've done better." Kalley groaned and squeezed her sister's hand.

"Did you leave a note for Richard so he'll know where to find you?" Carol asked.

"No," Kalley moaned as she limped toward the car.

Carol scribbled a note to Richard. "Kalley has gone into labor. She will be at Yale New Haven. Hurry if you'd like to see your baby born." She sniffed and tucked the note into the knocker.

Shortly after they arrived at the hospital, Keith sprinted down the corridor in his New Haven Fire Department uniform, walkie-talkie in hand. Hours later, Richard showed up with his mom, who carried several stuffed animals and three mylar balloons.

Carol and Keith introduced themselves to her. "I'm Keith, this is my wife Carol, and this is our other daughter, Lisa." Richard introduced his mom. "This is my mom. Her name is Nancy McCall." They all shook hands.

Kalley's labor stretched longer and longer, and in the twelfth hour Richard finally went into the birthing suite to check on her.

"Richard, about time you got here," Kalley screamed out between pains and pants, but she was relieved to see him. She didn't want her parents to know he had been gone for three days. She was grateful her mother had left the note, and that he had stopped by the house. The timing had worked out, but he could easily have missed the birth. He only stopped in once every three or four days, and it might have been pure luck that he'd come by that day.

Richard stood and watched, halfway between wonder and horror, as Kalley pushed when the nurse told her to push and rested when she had to. Kalley bit onto a cold rag and pushed harder.

She tried to think about anything else, but the pain brought her through memories of the preceding months. She had been miserable most of her pregnancy, but she'd tried not to make anything seem like a big deal. She didn't want Richard to think anything was wrong, she didn't want her parents to feel her fear, and she wanted to show herself that she could handle it all. But many days she secretly wished she hadn't gotten pregnant—that she hadn't even trusted Richard for anything other than clothes and jewelry.

"Richard went with me and bought the baby's crib," she had told her parents, knowing she bought the crib by herself, even though Richard had given her the money.

Richard made excuses about needing to call people and needing to go to the bathroom whenever Kalley screamed the loudest and cussed the hardest. Keith sent him back in to be with Kalley for the birth, but he soon left again. Carol stayed to coach and comfort Kalley.

The rest of the family sat in the waiting room. Seven hours after the twelfth hour of labor, Kalley finally seemed to make substantial progress. When Kalley was about to deliver, Carol ran out and told Richard, "Come in here so you can see your baby being born." Finally, nearly an hour later, the nurse came out and announced the arrival of a healthy baby boy.

Carol joined Keith, Lisa, and Nancy as soon as she knew Kalley was okay. "The baby is beautiful. He's six pounds. His name is Richard, after his dad, his middle name is Keith after his grandfather."

"Richard Keith McCall," Keith repeated. The four of them stood in the waiting room, each immersed in their own thoughts of being new grandparents and for Lisa, at becoming an aunt at age sixteen.

Carol winked at Keith. "Here is the son you told God you wanted." Lisa asked, "When will we be able to see Kalley and Little Rich?"

Everyone smiled. "Li'l Rich," Nancy said. "I like that."

"The nurse said she'd come and get us as soon as they finish cleaning her and the baby up." Carol replied.

⤏═◉ ◉═⤎

For a while, Kalley and Richard were alone in the nursery room with Li'l Rich. After they wheeled Kalley and the baby back to the recovery room, the family visited. Li' Rich was strong enough to stay in the room with Kalley overnight.

Nancy could hardly contain her excitement. "This is my first grandchild!" she said giddily. "He looks just like Richard did when he was born!"

Although she didn't say it aloud, she seemed surprised that it was Richard's baby. A few years earlier, another girl had said she was pregnant by Richard, but a DNA test showed her baby wasn't Richard's. Plus, the baby hadn't looked anything like Richard. This time, though, there was no doubt.

Carol walked in as Kalley was saying to Richard, "He's so little. He looks just like you, Richard." Richard stuck his chest out proudly, and Carol turned away slowly. "He reminds me of you when you were a baby," Carol said softly to Kalley. Her eyes moistened as she gazed down at the baby. He already had a head full of hair.

"He's going to be able to stay in the room with me tonight." Kalley smiled. She finally had a tiny man who would sleep next to her all night long, every night, no matter what.

"My how things have changed," Carol remarked. "He's absolutely beautiful. Perfect."

"Thanks, Mom. I don't know what I would have done without you," Kalley whispered, hugging Carol with one arm.

Carol had been praying the entire time that her daughter and grandchild would get through the ordeal safely. "Thank you, Lord for her safe delivery. But, Kalley, you did it without any help or drugs. I'm proud of you."

Actually, Carol was amazed that Kalley, at eighteen, had given birth without a C-Section or an epidural.

Lisa came in. "He's beautiful, Kalley," she said as she held her nephew and unwrapped the blanket, just as the parents and grandparents had just done to examine his toes and fingers.

Richard and Kalley beamed at each other proudly.

Just before everyone was about to leave, Keith pulled Richard aside. "Let's take a walk and have a little father-to-son talk." The two men went off away from the group.

"Congratulations, Richard. My grandson is beautiful."

"Thank you. Thank God the tough part's over!"

"Being a father and husband is the most difficult and important job you'll ever have. Learn to be a parent now, while it's easy, because it only gets tougher. If you do well as it gets tougher, it also gets more rewarding."

Richard shifted his weight. "Yeah," he said, searching for something else to add.

"Speaking of tough jobs," Keith continued, "Did you graduate from high school?"

"No, I'll go back next year and finish up."

"Well, I certainly hope so."

"Yes, sir."

Richard watched the vein in Keith's neck as it pulsed a little harder. Keith's voice gained momentum. "The primary reason I wanted to talk to you is I worry about my daughter."

"I can take care of my family."

Keith ignored his remark and continued. "How?" Keith asked frankly. "How are you going to support them? You now have a baby to feed and bills to pay. Neither of them can wait until you figure out your next hustle."

"I have a little money saved up. It will carry us until one of the jobs I applied for comes through."

"Pardon my French, young man, but let's call it what it is. You and I both know that's bullshit. You dropped out. You sell drugs, and you probably have for a while. If anything happens to my daughter or my grandson, I hold you responsible and you will have to deal with me."

"I really am trying to find work," Richard protested.

"It's not that I'm wishing you ill or hoping you fail, Richard," Keith said with a glimmer of firm love. "If you really do want to change, I'm right here. Come to me if you mean business. I know a few people that could help put you on the right track and help you with a job—a good job that you can build into a good life."

Suddenly, Richard's eyes narrowed and his voice went reedy. "I've been fending for myself ever since the beginning of high school without any help from anyone, especially a father figure, and I don't need one now." He threw his head back and stomped back to the waiting room.

"Mom, are you ready?"

"Yeah, I've been sitting here dozing, waiting for you," she replied.

"Kalley, I'll be back after I drop Mom off." Kalley rolled toward the window side of the room and sighed inaudibly.

→━◉ ◎━←

After Kalley gave birth, Carol and Keith had mixed feelings. On the one hand, they were happy about their healthy grandson. They'd been there through the whole process, and they'd already fallen in love with Li'l Rich. His cry seemed gentle and sweet, and his face reminded them of both Kalley and Richard.

Although they'd had dreams of walking Kalley down the aisle at her wedding, and visions of Keith giving her away to an established, Christian man, they realized they had one basic choice: they could be mostly happy or mostly angry. Of course, they still had deep misgivings about Richard. But they decided to pour their dreams into their new grandson's life, and not worry so much about Richard. Kalley could still find someone else—maybe not being married to Richard would turn out to be a blessing. She was still young, after all.

→━◉ ◎━←

"Hey, babe," Keith called as he came through the front door. "Where are you?"

"I'm in the kitchen," Carol called out. She was cooking dinner and had baked a peach cobbler for Kalley, who was doing well with everything except the hospital food.

Keith recounted his conversation with Richard. Keith ended with, "He's not ready for help, and I have a bad feeling that he's going to be ready for it right when there's none that can save him."

"You're an incredible husband and an amazing father. He would have gained more than he can understand if he had trusted you."

Keith sighed and smiled as he laid his hand on Carol's shoulder. "They say it is better to build children than it is to try to repair men. What they don't mention is that it's still better to repair men than to let death or jail work on them. I just hope it's better to try to repair men than to assume they can't be repaired."

Carol fixed Keith's plate and set it before him. "I talked to Nancy while the two of you were gone. She said that Richard always felt like he had to take care of things, even when his father left. He's been bitter ever since."

"That explains it, at least."

"Let's go see that new grandbaby," Carol teased, trying to lift Keith's mood. "It looks like you finally got the little boy you wanted."

Keith smiled sheepishly. "You think they'd let me put the little boy nursery together in our house for when he comes to visit and stay with us?"

"Small victories," Carol said. "Let's ask before we do anything, and try to act as if it's no big deal."

Keith and Carol arrived at Kalley's room. They knocked and stepped inside, where they saw Kalley staring out the window. Li'l Rich slept peacefully in a hospital bassinet next to her bed.

"He didn't come back after he dropped his mom off last night," Kalley murmured. "He didn't call this morning." She turned to look at her parents. "I've been worried sick about him."

Carol nudged Keith. Keith cleared his throat. "Richard runs the streets night and day and that is the way he chooses to live his life. He's been that way for a long time, long before he met you."

Kalley turned away and gazed out the window again.

Carol took Kalley's hand and patted it gently.

"Take the money he gives you and pay all the bills you can with it," Carol instructed. "Save whatever we give you and don't touch it."

Kalley's lip did not quiver; her eyes did not blink; her throat didn't tense. Her face became an African mask that Carol recognized all too well, and Carol suddenly stepped back and sat down in a bedside chair. Keith walked to the window side of the room and quietly pulled up another chair.

"You're a mother now," he said, "And we love you too much not to tell you the whole truth." Keith's tone of voice became very serious. "You, more than anyone else, should mainly focus on you and your child. We hope at some point you won't allow Richard's business to go on in or near your home, near you or your child." He paused to let it sink in, then continued. "Every dog has its day, but every one of those days comes to an end. Every last one."

"Dad, Richard is going to step up and be a good father. He's going to get a job. You just wait and see."

Carol and Keith exchanged a glance. Their hands met silently and their grip tightened, then relaxed as their hands withdrew.

Carol lifted the baby from the bassinet and began to sing "It Is Well With My Soul" slowly and richly. Carol's voice did not waver; her hands did not shake; yet, a tiny pair of tears slowly crested her eyelids and ran down her face, and she turned toward the window, holding Li'l Rich in the afternoon sunlight, just like her mother had done so many years ago when her father was in Vietnam.

⇥▸ ◂⇤

Kalley's godfather, Charles, whose cousin owned Tre Scalini, gave Kalley a job waiting tables and tending bar at the popular Italian restaurant. Kalley worked from 11 a.m. until 5 p.m. Her parents helped her, watching Li'l Rich on their days off. When they weren't available, they hired a babysitter. Kalley also kept her promise by taking some basic college courses three nights a week. That made Keith and Carl proud, but even that wasn't their favorite development.

To their surprise, Kalley seemed to take excellent care of Li'l Rich. Carol tactfully gave parental advice whenever she saw a minor shortcoming, but it wasn't as often as she or Keith had expected. Kalley seemed happy, and some days even relieved, to no longer want or need to chase the social spotlight. There was something about being a mother that brought her down to earth and gave her a new level of satisfaction.

Kalley drove to her parents' house to pick up Li'l Rich after her shift ended. *Has it really been a year already?* she wondered as her hands and feet guided the car automatically through the back streets. *Every day since Li'l Rich was born has gone by so fast! He's gotten so big..."* Her face soured as the wondered if Richard felt the same way about the past year. A smile crept back as she thought of her family. *Dad and Mom just worship the ground Li'l Rich walks on. "Sissy Auntie" Lisa spoils him rotten. She always brings him something new, and every week she takes him to the library for the children's story hour.* As she sat at a red light, thinking about some of the other girls in her senior class who had been pregnant—nobody had known at the time— she exhaled slowly and audibly. Those other girls were living at home with no car, no job, and no college courses.

Kalley used her key to open the front door.

"Mom, Dad, I'm back," she called.

"How was work?" Carol called out, walking toward Kalley with Li'l Rich on her hip.

"It was pretty busy. I had a good section," she smiled. "And Chris said if I keep doing well, I can expect a raise and management training—well, provided I keep taking business classes at night."

"You know your Dad and I have been so proud of you," Carol beamed. "You did all right."

"Mommy!" Li'l Rich raised his arms and gazed toward Kalley's face. She kissed him on the head and hugged him.

"I'm so happy to see my little man! I missed you."

He giggled and turned his face up for a kiss on his little lips. "Momma, ah wuv ooh."

"I love you, too, baby."

"Dad's working tomorrow," Carol said, "and I'll get in a little later. Tomorrow he goes to the sitter."

CHAPTER 27

A Family Tragedy

Time Indicator Here

CAROL AND KEITH were young among grandparents, only in their forties. They didn't mind a bit, though. In fact, they enjoyed Li'l Rich even more than they'd enjoyed Kalley and Lisa.

Li'l Richard was all boy, and he wore them out. Nonetheless, they loved chasing after him. Keith roughhoused with his grandson, which he'd never gotten to do with his girls. Carol would just look on and think, *The Lord works in mysterious ways.*

Kalley had grown much closer to Keith and Carol. Sometimes she would suddenly remember another special thing her mother had done with her as a little girl. She tried her best to imitate Carol's habits by reading to Li'l Rich often, singing songs as they walked and drove, and rocking him to sleep at night. And for the first time, Kalley knew her parents glowed with love for her as well as for Li'l Rich.

Of course, there was still Richard. She still had sex with him when he visited, but it wasn't the same as before Li'l Rich. Kalley kept her birth control pills hidden and never missed a day.

⊷⊫◉ ◉⊰⊶

One day, Kalley asked her mother, "Mom, did I talk early like Li'l Rich?"

Carol laughed reminiscently. "Yes indeed," she affirmed. "You were very smart. You even helped take care of Lisa one day when I was sleeping. You used to say, 'This my baby sister.'"

Kalley finished the last of an oatmeal cookie and wondered how Lisa was doing. Former tensions had eased between Kalley and Lisa. It helped that Lisa sometimes babysat Li'l Rich, whom she adored. Everything seemed so different.

⇥⊨◉ ◉⊨⇤

Late one Saturday afternoon, while Keith was still at work, Carol thawed steaks, fired up the grill, prepared baked potatoes, and boiled water while she shucked corn. "Gonna surprise the hardworkin' hubby," she smiled gently as she tossed husks into the garbage.

Lisa had gone to the movies with Betty. They planned to have dinner together at Betty's place afterward. Kalley was at home with Li'l Rich—she's just gotten off the phone with Carol. Sure, Li'l Rich only knew how to say four words anyone else would understand, but that didn't prevent them from having wonderful little talks! Carol hummed softly to herself as she prepared the evening meal.

Carol dropped the last ear of corn into the bubbling water. There was a flash of pain through her left arm, and then it was gone. She rubbed her arm and shook her head. She'd never felt anything like it before, like a lightning strike inside her body, there and then gone in the same instant.

She laughed and stepped over to the steaks. She was about to pick them up when an overwhelming tightness gripped her chest. She leaned on her arm and breathed shallowly. Sometimes she had acid reflux, and the gas pains sometimes gave her the same feeling, just not as bad. She decided to get her anti-acid medicine.

By the time she reached the second stair, another sudden sharp pain shot across her left arm. "Oh, God," she choked out. Something heavy descending, and then crushing weight—she turned back and made it to the kitchen phone, where she tried to hurry up, *hurry up, dial the number, there's only three digits. Nine, then reach up and left, no, further, reach for it, you can do it—good! One. Now release it, pull back the finger, Carol, hurry, let go, so you can press it again,* but her finger was suddenly heavier than everything, and she couldn't stop pressing the button, and she slumped forward, her head hitting several numbers at once as she crumpled.

The receiver bungee-jumped, springing up just before reaching the linoleum floor, and then falling again, springing up, and falling again, less and less each time, until it finally dangled motionless on the end of its cord.

"Keith," she wheezed as the lights got dimmer and dimmer, so quickly, and suddenly even the earth was swallowed in the vast expanse of space, where not even one distant star lit her path home.

Keith was not a superstitious man, and he certainly didn't trust "gut instinct." He felt an emotional jolt, though, that he couldn't explain; it was far beyond intuition. He dialed the house number on the firehouse phone, but the line was busy. He kept calling every few minutes. Still busy.

Betty's mom was pruning her azaleas when she heard the smoke detector's distant shriek. At first, she didn't give it a thought. But after it continued to blare for fifteen minutes, she put down her pruning shears, took off her gloves, and walked toward the sound.

When she saw Carol's car in the driveway, she ran to the Davidsons' door, the high-pitched whine getting louder with every step.

"Carol!" she called out. No one answered the door. "Carol!!" she yelled, pounding the door. She trotted around to the back of the house and saw thick darkness pressing against the kitchen window. She grabbed her phone and quickly dialed 911.

Keith's station heard the call over their radio system. "Shit!" Keith hissed, slamming the receiver down and sprinting toward the trucks. Rubin grabbed him by the arm. "Bro, that's not even our district. Don't even—"

Keith's radio crackled, and the two men froze as the dispatcher announced "smoke sighted" and stated the address twice. Rubin's grip tightened. "Stay put," he said forcefully, spinning and joining the sprint toward the trucks. "I will take care of it!"

Keith wanted to take one of the company fire cars or even his car and rush home, but he had to follow company protocol and wait for the chief to come to drive him home, and leave his car at the station.

Finally the chief came, and he drove Keith home. Neither spoke as they got nearer and nearer the pillar of ashy smoke. Keith mouthed, "Let Carol be all right, Lord. I know she's going to be all right."

When they arrived at the scene, Carol's body was on a stretcher in front of the house. A small cloud of medics with a defibrillator tried to revive her. As Keith jumped out of the car and sprinted over, a policeman stopped him and asked him who he was. The medical crew loaded the stretcher into the ambulance, and the officer let Keith climb in as well.

One of the EMTs, Dave, updated Keith. It seemed that Carol had knocked the phone off the hook while trying to call for help because from where she lay on the floor, the phone was right beside her.

Dave kept talking long after Keith's ears started to shut out the sounds around him. He looked down at the stretcher, which seemed to jounce very heavily with every bump and turn.

At the hospital, the medics wheeled the stretcher into the maze of corridors. Keith sat stoically in the waiting room until a doctor called him over. "We couldn't save her," he said in a hushed tone. "By the time the team arrived, it was already too late."

Keith fell to his knees and pounded the floor. Tears rained down alongside his fists, and after a few minutes he slumped forward. The nurses on duty helped him into a chair.

Fifteen long minutes later, Keith asked, "May I see my wife?" His arms ached and his hands throbbed, but they also seemed very far away.

"They will have her cleaned up in a little while and we'll come and get you," replied a nurse. Keith nodded, pulling another sob down and drowning it in the depths of his churning stomach.

When Lisa, Betty, and her parents arrived, they spotted Keith in the waiting area with one of his fire buddies and one of the EMS crew. Keith's head hung down, tears rolling down his face to his fingers and wrist.

"Daddy?" Lisa asked gently as she reached his side.

Keith looked up and wrapped Lisa in his arms. "Mom's in a better place."

Lisa, usually the family stoic, broke into tears and couldn't stop crying. Keith and she cried together, their heavy breaths pulsing together and then in contrast.

"Does Kalley know?" Betty asked, as she patted Lisa on the back, trying to comfort her.

Keith shook his head. "I'm going to tell her in person."

Keith and Lisa caught a ride with Betty's family to get their car from the station's parking lot, then they all drove to Kalley's place.

When they arrived, Kalley's car was parked in the apartment lot, but not Richard's. This time, that made Keith glad. He took a deep breath, then knocked on the door.

As soon as Kalley opened the door, she blurted, "Where's Mom? You have never come over without her." She craned her neck around Keith to see who was in the car. She could see that Lisa was in the car, and behind it, a second car with Betty and her parents. In the third car was Dave, Dad's buddy from work.

"Daddy, what's wrong?" Kalley asked. "Where's Mom? You're scaring me."

Keith just hugged her. "Make sure Li'l Rich has his coat. I'll explain in the car."

As she walked up to the car window, holding her baby, she saw Lisa sitting in the passenger seat. She was weeping.

"Daddy, what's the matter?" Kalley pleaded.

Kalley climbed in the back seat. She strapped little Richard in the extra car seat that Keith and Carol kept there for convenience when they babysat.

"Where's Mom?"

Keith had hoped the news could wait, but he relented. "Mom had a heart attack." Keith was fighting back tears as he talked.

"What hospital is she in? Let's go see her."

"It was a massive heart attack," Keith said. "She didn't make it."

"No." Kalley was in total disbelief and shock.

"She was home alone. It happened so fast nothing could be done."

"Where was everyone?" Kalley shouted indignantly.

"Lisa and Betty had gone to see a show. I was at work. It happened this evening when she was cooking dinner."

"But we just talked to her this evening. She said she was going to surprise you and take your favorite dinner to the station. She even talked with Li'l Rich!"

As the news sunk in, Kalley cried so hard that Li'l Rich started crying. Soon, everyone was weeping and sobbing.

Keith pulled over to the curb, and Betty's Dad had to pull his car over and park as well. He came over to the car to check on the bereaved family.

Everyone was talking at once as the shock soaked in.

As things settled down, Kalley turned to Lisa. "You're always home. Why tonight would you take off? Tonight of all times?" Lisa turned toward the window and didn't look at Kalley.

CHAPTER 28

Family Grief

The Next Day

THE NEXT DAY Keith called his family and Kim's family to break the news. The family made hasty travel arrangements while Keith coordinated the funeral. After speaking with the funeral director, Keith stood in Carol's closet, looking at all the dresses, skirts, and blouses and remembering what they'd been doing when she'd last worn each of them. He touched a few of the blouses, and drew one to his face, inhaling the latent scent of Carol's favorite perfume.

Finally, tearstained and tired, Keith gathered Kalley and Lisa. "Pick out something nice for Mommy to wear. Then make a short list of what we need to do to get the house ready. You'll be the main greeters and hostesses."

The girls picked out Carol's favorite white suit. They were concerned about how it would highlight the unusual darkness of her left hand, but they still liked the outfit. Lisa phoned the funeral home and asked if it would be possible to have Carol's hand made up to a more natural hue.

Keith went back to the bedroom and took Carol's bathrobe off the hook behind the bathroom door. He lay on the bed, his head resting on the collar of the robe, remembering all the times he'd nuzzled Carol's shoulders and kissed her neck. More tears, and then Keith got up, grabbed his keys, and called out, "I'm going for a drive. Gotta clear my head."

As he drove around, Keith spoke to Carol in low tones. "Honey, did you stop taking your heart medication? You were supposed to continue taking them until the doctor told you to stop. What are we supposed to do without you? We need you. How are we supposed to go on?"

Keith looked down at his handwritten list:

- Funeral Home
- Flower shop
- Insurance papers filed
- Request death certificate

"I have got to stay busy, babe," he muttered, "Or I'm going to lose it completely."

At home, Lisa and Kalley began receiving friends they knew from work, from First Baptist, and from school. Everyone who arrived brought homemade food. Carol's students sent cards and visited with their parents. They dropped off food, flowers, and cash gifts tucked into greeting cards. All gave heartfelt condolences and asked the girls, "What can we do to help?"

Reverend Sewell, the associate pastor at First Baptist, was so distraught he could hardly speak. He and his wife retreated to the upstairs bathroom to pray for release from their emotions. They came down a little while later and continued to comfort the family. In the living room, glutted with chairs brought from other parts of the house and other houses in the neighborhood, Reverend Sewell remarked, "Carol gave all that she had to everyone. I guess her heart had been so big she couldn't carry it any longer."

Within two days, Keith's Mom and siblings arrived. Richard's mother, Nancy, brought Richard's sister with her to the funeral, but there was no sign of Richard. Kalley said he'd called once or twice but didn't know whether or not to expect him.

⤜●═●⤛

Kim and her family arrived first. She stepped right in and took the lead on arranging the burial, funeral, and repast. She even arranged the dinner at the church with the girls to keep them busy after the cemetery burial. All of the family members and friends tried to help Keith relax. The busier he became, the more they tried to slow him down.

Lisa asked her friend Marsha to sing her mom's favorite song at the funeral, Cece Wynans's "Don't Cry for Me." Kalley helped her dad assemble the program together.

The service and the funeral were held at First Baptist, which was full to overflowing. Kim broke down in the middle of her eulogy; two ushers escorted her to the church basement to regroup.

Richard arrived late. He walked up beside Kalley and took her hand. Betty stayed by Lisa while her parents held Li'l Rich.

Keith tried to keep a stoic face, but he sat, winged by Lisa and Kalley and surrounded by twenty firemen in dress uniform. After the service, the interment at the cemetery, and the repast at the church, the family returned to the house. Carol's friends stayed with the family at the house and ate, talked, and played gospel music.

"Keith, I think you should take some more time off because I think you're not ready for work yet," Gwen told him.

Keith nodded somberly. "I don't think I'm going back yet. That would mean leaving Lisa home by herself. Some weeks I'm gone three or four nights straight."

"Dad, pretty soon I'll be out on my own, so until then I will be all right here at home alone," Lisa assured him.

Betty's family gave Lisa a key. "If she wants to stay at our house overnight when you work, she can," Betty's father assured Keith. Betty wrapped her arm around Lisa's waist and added, "I can come over when you want to sleep in your own bed, Lisa, and stay on the couch."

"Betty, that is so sweet." Lisa hugged her friend.

"I spend half my time over here anyway." Betty smiled.

Keith smiled. "Thank you all." He moved a little slower than usual as he climbed the stairs to get Betty a spare key, gripping the banister firmly and half-pulling himself to each successive step.

CHAPTER 29

Life Without Carol

AS TIME WENT on, the family adjusted to Carol's absence. Everyone carried a sore and heavy heart, but life went on.

Late one afternoon, Kalley let herself into her parents' house to find a few pictures. She went through the tiny frames cascading across the serving table looking for the portrait Lisa had taken of Kalley and of her parents on Kalley's graduation day. Then she scoured the collection for the shot of Li'l Rich and Betty that Carol had taken when Li'l Rich was just a few days old.

On a whim, Kalley wandered up to her parents' room and found a picture of Li'l Rich and her mother in a silver frame on the end table. It sat right near where Carol used to lay her head every night. She remembered there was an identical print in the den, on the mantle over the fireplace. Kalley went down into the den and held the duplicate picture in her hand.

Lisa heard someone moving around the house. She went downstairs and found her sister. "Hi, how's everything going?"

"Okay," Kalley said hollowly. Lisa's heart sank. One word into the conversation, and Kalley sounded exhausted.

"Oh, okay. I heard somebody, but I thought it was Betty," Lisa said softly, turning toward the stairs.

"No movies tonight for the two of you?" Kalley asked bitterly.

Lisa turned and looked back toward Kalley. "Don't start. Leave that alone."

"Don't tell me what to do. You can't take the truth that Mom could have still been here if it wasn't for you."

Lisa went back into the den and almost stood on Kalley's toes. She stared firmly at her sister, eyes inches apart.

Kalley swung and hit Lisa on the left side of her face. In an instant, the melee was on. Carol's Tiffany lamp spewed jagged Technicolor snowflakes of broken glass across the tan oak floor. Picture frames buckled and splintered as Kalley smashed the glass panes against Lisa's head, deforming the images of Carol and the family. A heavy glazed potting jar with a withering stem smashed against the brick outline of the fireplace, and soil exploded back into the room.

Lisa tackled Kalley hard, driving her back until she sprawled across the card table where Carol used to put together the jigsaw puzzles with their impossibly tiny pieces. Lisa fell on top of Kalley, buckling the table legs and letting them all fall with a crunch. Lisa's right hand throttled Kalley, whose eyes bulged.

"Oh, you wanna talk trash? Be real, now," Lisa growled. "Did you ever think about the trouble you caused Mom and Dad back in the day? That surely didn't help her heart any."

Suddenly, Lisa drew her hand back, and Kalley's throat rasped as she inhaled. Pushing herself up, Lisa turned and walked up the stairs.

Kalley grabbed the marble bookend from the bookshelf and sprinted to catch up. With no warning, she swung it at Lisa with all her force. Lisa started to duck but didn't get clear of the bookend in time. Her body went limp and flopped down the three stairs into the den.

"Oh, no, no, no…" Kalley dropped the bookend, which thudded twice on the carpet. She scurried down the stairs and prodded Lisa with her foot. "Oh, Jesus," Kalley mumbled. "Oh, God, what the hell did I do?" She ran her hands through her hair, over her temples and behind her ears, over and over again. She sprinted out the door, revved the car, and tore off down the street.

Fortunately, Betty was home and heard a car spin off recklessly. When she reached the window, she saw the tail end of Kalley's car flying down the street. Betty sprinted across the lawn.

"Lisa!!" she called as she looked up the stairs. A weary voice drew Betty's attention to the lower landing. "Betts… down here."

Betty whipped out her phone and dialed 911. After trying to explain to the dispatcher that she couldn't just stay on the line, she hung up on her and called

Keith at the station. "Lisa's hurt. I found her on the floor in the den. The para-medics are on the way. Meet us at Yale."

⇥⊙ ⊙⇤

Keith held Lisa's hand as the nurse applied butterfly stitches to the back of Lisa's head.

"That's it," Keith said grimly. "She's gone too far now."

Lisa winced. "Dad, don't do anything to her," she said one word at a time in between needle sweeps. "I shouldn't have choked her."

After the stitches were complete, Keith drove straight to Kalley's house. When he arrived, he pounded on the door like a policeman would. Kalley let him in wordlessly.

"What is wrong with you?" Keith fumed. "Do you need to see a therapist? Nobody is comfortable without Mom; nobody. But we're not going to start kill-ing each other over it. This ends here and now."

Kalley crossed her arms across her chest.

"Something's wrong with you for blaming your sister for what happened. I thought we got this straight the night of Mommy's death. You keep blaming your sister for not being home. Ask yourself why you weren't there. That answer is much more complex. But I have to face it, too. I wasn't there, either. As much as it tears me up to admit this, it was simply Carol's time. I didn't want it to be, you didn't want it to be, and your sister didn't want it to be, either. You will go and apologize to your sister, and you will never strike a blood relative again."

Kalley had never seen her dad so mad, but she held her ground. "I'm not apologizing because she came at me first. She started the fight."

"So that meant fight to the death?!" Keith howled.

"She tried to choke me out."

"She already admitted she was wrong to fight. It's not right for either of you. Everything about this situation was wrong, and I have to take measures. Give me your house key."

Kalley reluctantly pressed the silvery key into her father's palm. He turned and walked out the door as Kalley railed at him from inside.

"If you want to take her side, I don't need to come over there. I got family right here."

She slammed the door as hard as she could, then spun and slumped down to meet her knees. She covered her face with both hands and gave a resigned moan. Richard hadn't been home in two weeks.

Kalley never set foot again in her parents' house. She let Keith pick up Li'l Rich every other weekend. She wouldn't call, and whenever her father called her, their conversations were dry and halting.

Kalley and Lisa didn't speak. Lisa's high school graduation was strained by the sisters' distance. Keith asked Lisa to call Kalley and invite her to the graduation, but Lisa refused. He sent Kalley an invitation but didn't hear back from her. That weekend, she didn't even open the door when Keith arrived at the usual time to pick up Li'l Rich.

He called a few days before Lisa's graduation ceremony. "Hi, Kalley. It's Daddy."

"Hi," came the cardboard reply.

"Lisa's graduation is Thursday night," he said, "and we want you and your family to attend the ceremony with us. Mom would have wanted us all together." After a few seconds, Keith heard a gentle click. He replaced the receiver slowly and shook his head. Graduation came and went with no sign of Kalley, Richard, or Li'l Rich.

When Lisa departed for college, Keith drove with her in Carol's car, which had become Lisa's. He helped get her settled in her new dorm room on the lush University of Virginia campus before flying home two days later.

CHAPTER 30

Lorraine and Richard

June 14, 2007

IN THE HEART of Farnam Courts, people swirled around in bright fuchsia, lime, and canary tones of spring, rejoicing to be free from coats and gloves and hats and reveling in early spring sunshine. Barbecue pits emitted rings of hickory-scented smoke as residents hungrily stoked the coals. The pall of poverty, dis-enfranchisement, and failed promises didn't hang so heavily on such fine spring afternoons. And since it was the first of the month, neighbors bought food and drink to share freely. The air tasted like hope, and they were all rich for the day.

Two women sat on a stoop, surrounded by the impromptu celebration. "Well, where you think he's at?" Kenisha asked her friend, Lorraine, leaning in.

"Ain't the first time he up and vanished. Been gone four days now. Said he couldn't stand the stress."

Lorraine was a slender five foot seven inch frame with bluish dark skin and the ashy highlights of a reformed drug-user. Healthy or not, these days she always looked tired and on the verge of illness. Her figure hinted at yes-teryear's enviable muscle tone and traffic-stopping Coca-Cola bottle curves. She walked with a thin metal cane that made a hollow sound when it tapped the sidewalk or the wall.

"Did you report him as a missing person?"

Lorraine slowly got up and laughed. "Aw, hell naw. And it ain't like the po-lice ever not lookin' for him. Come on now; you know what it is. He all held up with some new piece that thinks he's the man." She sneered and her voice rose contemptuously. "You know how he can front when he first meets a female."

"Yeah, I know that's right."

"He's a straight up dog." She paused. "Like my nana used t'say, a fool is a fool. He gonna show his ass before it's over."

"Anyway, if he has any work on him and the police bust him we all goin' down. Not me, though, not this time. Nuh uh. I'm staying clean."

Kenisha thought about it. "Yeah, wouldn't be long 'fore they bustin' down the door at your place."

"That fool throwing bricks at the jail."

Lorraine's temper was starting to flare as she thought about the situation. "He knows the rent past due. As always, he know I'm'a figure it out, so he get ghost an' let me figure it out."

"I can front you a little if you want."

"Thanks, but I took care of it. Richard doesn't know it's paid." She sucked her teeth.

"The usual?" asked Kenisha.

"I ain't proud of it, but keep it a buck, girl. It's there whenever I need it. It's there whenever any half-decent girl needs it, and with these little boys running in and out of our lives that's a good thing. These boys be calling themselves men, right? And they wanna wear the boxer shorts until it's time to be the man, then they want to panty up and be the bitch. They want to have the balls, yet wear the drawers."

"Girl, you crazy. You and Richard go back! Y'been with him since high school, right?"

"I know. But one of these days he's gonna come home and it's just gonna be empty. I'm not always gonna be there for him. The only reason I've stayed is because he was my first and when I been sick, he has come through then."

"Why you gotta be sick for him to treat you right?"

Lorraine didn't answer. "Come on, girl. Let's go get some barbecue."

CHAPTER 31

A World on Her Shoulders

FOUR WOMEN, TWO houses, and one full-time street hustle stretched Richard thin. He told Kalley things were tough because she somehow always seemed to fend for herself. Their savings had been depleted six months prior, rent had been overdue for one month, and Kalley kept re-negotiating her deal with the utility company.

Everything had started to go sideways when Richard got busted on the way back from New York City. A Connecticut State Trooper pulled him over for illegal tints in the Honda. The trooper's dog found a half a kilo of cocaine and nine hundred dollars. The car got towed. Kalley bonded him out and give Richard a few dollars to try to flip, hoping he'd get back to helping her. Effectively, though, they just lived on Kalley's income and shared her car.

"Richard, my car isn't going to last much longer if we don't get it repaired soon. Do you think you'll have any money coming in today?"

"Don't pressure me. You see I'm doing the best I can right now."

"I dropped my college classes so I could work longer hours to help and let you keep the car longer. I'm not bugging you, Boo, it's just we're using the car twice as much, the babysitter charges more with me being gone longer. We're just barely keeping the lights and gas on. I just don't know what to do."

"We'll be okay. Just keep hanging in there with me. It's gonna turn around."

"How? What are you going to do to turn it around?"

"Listen. It's time to go get Li'l Rich from the babysitter. Can you see if your dad can keep him this weekend?"

"I don't want to impose on him. It's good he still keeps him every other weekend, considering he and I barely talk. He and Lisa send clothes and toys, too."

Richard sighed. "I ain't gonna make no money sitting in here with Li'l Rich, don't matter how many clothes and toys he has."

Kalley opened the door, then turned. "You coming?"

"Nah," Richard replied. "I'll be here when you get back."

After Kalley left, Richard went outside, grabbed a bag from his pocket and lit up. He inhaled. Things were going to get better. He didn't need to sleep; he could work all night.

→══● ●══←

The next day, Kalley picked up the phone and dialed the familiar number.

"Dad, can I come over and talk to you?"

"Sure, baby girl. My door is always open."

Kalley came alone. After a few minutes of pleasantries, she sat down on the couch and broke down crying. "Daddy, I'm so sorry."

At first, Keith didn't say anything. He just patted her back and caressed her. After a minute, he said, "I already forgave you a long time ago. I just needed to hear what I've just heard from you."

After she calmed down, she explained everything from what happened to Richard to how they were living. "I dropped out of my classes to try and help, but we're just going down the financial tubes."

He looked at his daughter with compassion before he spoke. "Kalley, the only way I can help is if you and Li'l Rich come back home to live, or if Richard lets me help find him a job. If he doesn't want that kind of help, then, frankly, put his no-good ass out."

"If it was just me and Li'l Rich, you would be there for us without hesitation. But if you've taught me anything about how to handle hard times, then you and I both know I can't put him out, good or not, when things are so hard. I will talk to him about taking a real job."

When Richard came home later that week, Kalley told him he needed to change his strategy. "I know it's not something you're used to doing, but you can stop sneaking around, and we won't need another car, and we can start getting things straight again. You know, saving?"

Richard exploded. "How the fuck is he gonna tell me how to take care of my family? You and your dad need to stop stepping into what you can't understand!" He kicked the tiny table in the dining room and the salt and pepper jumped off. The saltshaker broke on the floor. Richard slammed the door and the whole apartment shook. Kalley looked at the tiny pillar of salt next to the broken saltshaker. She heard tires screeching and shook her head. She called her friend Meshell and asked for a ride to work.

After drinking a glass of water, Kalley called her dad back. "Dad, I'm sorry. Richard should have said yes, but he got offended and ran off with the car."

"Whatever you and Li'l Rich need, I'll get it and drop it off. And when the car turns up, send it to the shop and have it fixed. Just have the mechanic call me before doing anything so I have an estimate. You and Li'l Rich need to be able to get around safely. Outside of that, though, you're on your own. You're staying with the man who is holding you down."

⤙▨◉ ◉▨⤚

Richard didn't come back. Nine months after storming out, Kalley got a collect call. The operator identified the call as coming from a state penitentiary, and she sighed and declined the call. There wasn't anything to explain to Richard, really. She smiled, picked up Li'l Rich, and gave him a kiss.

CHAPTER 32

Alzheimer Strikes
The Family

NOT LONG AFTER accepting a commission as lieutenant, Keith started to forget small details more and more often. It was nothing he couldn't fix—he could always check and see whether or not his toothbrush was wet so he'd know whether or not he'd already brushed his teeth on a given morning. He could always look at the wall calendar to see what day it was. Keith battled alone and tried not to let on to anyone else about his struggles with day-to-day memory and routines.

As months passed, he would sometimes lock himself out of the house or leave his keys in the car with the car still running long after he'd gone inside and gotten ready for bed. He even lost track of time, especially after dark, and could not remember what time it was or what days he was scheduled to work.

Eventually, though, everyone started to notice Keith's waning awareness. He started going to the wrong car in the parking lot. One day he walked into the grocery store across the street from the fire station and asked what they'd done with the trucks. One night, he had to show a Southern Connecticut State security guard his driver's license and get written directions home.

The boys at the station finally staged a quick intervention. Rubin and Charles went into Keith's office to talk with him. "Keith, man, you're slipping. We're worried about you. Let us make you an appointment for some medical tests." Keith didn't need to be coerced; he let them call the doctor's office immediately.

After the evaluation, Keith opted for early retirement. He had early on-set Alzheimer's disease. Fortunately, it wasn't in its latter stages. It still cycled through better weeks, when Keith could still function independently, before a bad stretch, in which Keith relied on other people very often.

Lisa had to take some time out of school to come back home to get things straightened out for her father. Keith and Lisa decided that since he didn't want to live in Virginia and she didn't want to move back to Connecticut, Keith would move into an assisted living facility. Keith felt humiliated at first, but after visiting several locations they found one with excellent services. Keith would still have access to his car—he'd just have a driver instead of driving himself—he'd live in a cottage instead of in the large full-time care building, and staff were on call 24/7 at the push of a button.

Keith's mental faculties improved once he began a new medication program. Lisa visited him every day and helped him get settled. They discussed Kalley's situation several times. Keith was adamant. "Kalley isn't in any condition to help me out—not as long as Richard is still in her life. Most of the time, it's not her fault, but it doesn't change the fact. Besides, she has enough on her hands with Li'l Rich."

The following month, Lisa sold the beautiful white colonial she and Kalley had grown up in. Her father instructed her, "Split the money between the two of you, but only send Kalley one thousand dollars a month until her half is paid."

"Dad, what do I need to send you?" she asked worriedly.

"With the policy from your mom and the insurance I have from my job, it will cover my stay and the medical expenses at my new place. I'm just fine. You go back to school and make something of yourself."

In his newfound clarity, Keith decided to start journaling. He'd researched Alzheimer's enough to understand it was progressive but also had unpredictable jumps, so he cherished every day when he could think coherently. He began keeping a journal about his life with Carol, so that when he could no longer remember, he would have his story to hand down to his daughters and grandson. He wrote the entire story, from their first day to her last.

⋆⟶⊜ ⊜⟵⋆

Kalley grabbed the mail from the mailbox and tossed it down on the passenger seat. She finally had her car back and in good working order. She still pingponged between elation and anger about that—it was wonderful to have the car, but she never should have had to go without it, either.

She cut the ignition, picked up the stack of mail, threw her purse over her shoulder, and walked up to the apartment. Li'l Rich was already asleep—the babysitter had texted an hour earlier—so she entered quietly, paid the sitter, and then went through the mail. Catalogs, credit card offers—didn't they know better by now?—and a hand-addressed envelope with Dad's name and a weird return address, none of it written in Dad's shaky handwriting.

She opened the envelope. Folded inside a blank piece of paper was a check for one thousand dollars. She compared the address to the return address on the envelope. They were the same, so Kalley picked up the check and repeated the number to herself softly. She went over to the phone and called Keith, who invited her and Li'l Rich to come over and see his new home.

→▷ ◁←

The next morning, as she drove to Keith's new address, Kalley shook her head. She had been working so hard; she'd been so busy shuttling Li'l Rich to school and to his grandmother's house and back home. The whole while, she'd had no idea what her dad had been going through.

Keith was happy to see Kalley. His memory was holding up well, as it had been for the past several days.

"Hey, Daddy," she said, hugging him and letting him hold her close. "What's going on?"

"Well, the times are changing, that's for sure. I got Alzheimer's disease. I noticed it a while back, and I tried to handle things privately. The guys at the station helped me for a little while, but eventually they told me what your mom would have told me from the start: to go get evaluated. Well, as you can see, when things get bad it's dangerous for me to be alone. Now that I have medications and staff around all the time, it's safer for everyone. I'm just glad I can be near you and Li'l Rich. C'mere, li'l man!"

Li'l Rich rushed into his grandfather's bear hug. Keith laughed and shook Li'l Rich gently. Kalley smiled. Keith looked up at her. "How are you doing?"

"Bad. I mean, good, like I'm working and taking care of everything, but..." she sighed, then shrugged, and continued. "Richard left. That happened right after you offered to help him find a job again. He's in jail. He called me—I didn't accept the call…"

Keith nodded and ambled over to the refrigerator. He took out a large glass pitcher brimming with dark ruby liquid. "Sweet tea?" he asked.

She nodded, blinking out some tears while Keith poured two tall glasses and one short one.

"You've learned," he said as he handed Kalley the iced tea.

"Yes, I've learned," she said achingly. "What I learned is that I was an idiot for a long time. You and Mom told me everything about Richard right from the start. You never knew him, but you knew anyway. And I just wouldn't listen. I kept hoping, I kept working, I kept trying, I kept praying. He's gone now. That's even a foolish thing to say, because he was gone before Li'l Rich was even born."

"I could have given you the house," Keith said wistfully. Kalley's eyebrows tented.

"The house? You could have given me the house?"

"Well, kinda," Keith said. "Maybe you and Li'l Rich could have moved in and maybe I could have gotten some in-home care when you weren't there."

Kalley sighed. "If I'd known Richard wasn't coming back—well, I don't know. I'm still stupid for him, Daddy. When he's not there, I miss him, and when he is there I wish he'd never come back. I might have done the right thing, but I can't really say. Sometimes, even when I know the right thing, I hang on to an idea that I can't really reach. But I still want it."

Keith nodded, sipped his tea, and smiled. "You know, I could spend a lot of time worrying about what I did and didn't do. I could worry about what I can and can't do, or what I will and won't be able to do in the future. But all that thinking brings me back to Reverend Bishop's favorite verse."

"Romans 8:28!" It was half groan and half exclamation, but nonetheless Kalley smiled.

Keith did his best Reverend Bishop impression. "And we know that in aaaaall things, God works for the good of those who love him, who have been called according to his purpose." Kalley laughed, and Li'l Rich laughed, and then Keith laughed. Keith reached out and touched Kalley's shoulder. "But you remember what he used to say after that?"

Kalley nodded quietly, and then she said softly, "The Word says, 'in all things,' not 'in some things' or 'in a few things,'" she recalled. "Even the things that are put into our path to hurt us get repurposed by God."

Keith's eyebrows rose. "I didn't even think you'd remember that!" he exclaimed. Kalley nodded and gazed into the distance. "It's one of the things I've never been able to forget or ignore, no matter how hard I tried."

CHAPTER 33

Kalley and Lisa as Adults

KALLEY FELT YOUNGER and happier again when she brought all her accounts current. She could hardly believe the rent was up to date, the utilities were taken care of, and her cell phone was even working again. She had Li'l Rich in after-school care, and she had registered for another semester of college. She went to school two nights a week and visited her father as much as possible.

She spent more time with Li'l Rich. He was in Pop Warner football and travel basketball, and she cheered loudly at every game. In the spring, she purchased a HUD-subsidized house in a middle-class area where all the kids played together during the day and went home by nine. It was a neighborhood rule, and Kalley liked it—it meant she and Li'l Rich got time to read and pray before bed.

-»╼═● ●═╾«-

"Where does the time go?" Lisa asked herself. The room was awash in graduation excitement. Lisa was seated on the side of an impossibly long table at Olive Garden with the rest of her information technology practicum team. They'd built an uncrackable data encryption code for their senior practicum, and they'd all gotten A's in the class and had job offers waiting for them. The girls laughed and drank and told their tales of struggles from the practicum and success in their job interviews, and Lisa sighed and sat back and closed her eyes for a moment. She was valedictorian—again—and would soon have a dual degree; she'd studied business management as well as IT. She was starting with the NSA the week after graduation, moving into her dream house in Washington, D.C., and trying to adjust to the idea of being on her own. Nothing was wrong, but life was still a constant challenge anyway. Stay on top of assignments, think ahead, plan, coordinate, exercise, eat well, and don't forget to sleep, but take some time for you— it was a miracle that nothing fell through the cracks. And she'd had to recover from taking the winter term off the year before to move her father into assisted care. She thought about her mother and father. Soon she'd be seeing him at graduation. As for Kalley, well, time would tell.

Dad had asked her to invite Kalley, of course, back when she moved him into the elder care center.

"Lisa, you know I don't ask you for much," he'd said gently. "I really feel it's important that you invite your sister when graduation comes around."

Lisa had smiled. "Dad, that'll be a night of new beginnings for me. My whole life I've tried to establish a relationship with my sister. It's never worked out. Are you really sure that isn't just going to deepen the rift between her and me?"

"Your mom would want you to try."

"Bringing out the Big Guns of Guilt, I see," she'd said with the hint of a grin. "Please tell me you've thought this through. Remember: it's my big night, and I won't be trying to have any mixed feelings or negative thoughts about the past. I see a lot of ways things could go wrong."

Keith had sat back and shaken his head. "I can't make you love or forgive her, and I can't make her love or forgive you," he'd admitted. "It doesn't mean I won't try. I'm going to talk with Kalley, when the time comes. If she reaches out to you, promise me you won't reject her. Let that be your sign that it's time for healing." He'd squeezed Lisa's hand so hard that Lisa winced.

"Okay, Dad." He hadn't let go. "Dad. Dad! You're squeezing my hand to death!" Keith had suddenly snapped out of the trance. He'd released Lisa's hand quickly and chided himself. "I am so sorry. Got lost in my thoughts again."

Lisa had smiled and rubbed her hand gingerly. "I know."

⇥⊙ ⊙⇤

Keith and Kalley ate sandwiches at the kitchen table. Li'l Rich had gone to bed, and Keith had toured the new house.

He was elated that Kalley had her own place, could afford everything, and was still able to do well in her night classes.

"I want you to do something for me," he said, reaching underneath his sweater to the breast pocket of his buttondown shirt.

"What is it?" Kalley asked.

Keith handed her an envelope. "Why don't you surprise your sister and go down to her graduation. A plane ticket and all the information is enclosed. We haven't been together as a family since your graduation."

Kalley half-scowled. "I want to make you happy, Daddy. But I also know, and I think you probably remember that my sister made it crystal clear: she doesn't want me there. There's a reason she sent one adult ticket and one child ticket, and sent them to you. That means you and Li'l Rich."

"Both of my daughters are beautiful and stubborn, just like their mother, may she rest in peace."

"When she sends the money every month, there's no return address on the envelope. That's another way she lets me know she doesn't want any contact. I'm just glad she included Li'l Rich because he doesn't have anything to do with our disagreement."

⇀⇁⊙ ⊙⇀⇁

Throughout his trip to Virginia, Keith always scanned the background to see if Kalley would appear. Li'l Rich looked for her, too, but after a few days he seemed to understand that she wasn't coming.

Keith and Li'l Rich stayed for four days and had a good time together with Lisa. When they returned, Keith gave Kalley a call. "We're back. You can take your time picking up Li'l Rich. Hold on, he wants to talk to you."

"Hi, Mom. We took lots of pictures at the graduation. Virginia is a really pretty state. We had a really good time. I only wish you had been there, Mom. It was not the same without you."

"I missed you too," Kalley said sweetly. "You are such a little charmer! Kiss, kiss. I love you, son."

"Don't rush, Mom. I want to spend some time with Granddad. Man talk." He handed the phone back to Keith.

"Kalley, see you whenever. We'll talk when you come over. Li'l Rich and I have some games to watch."

As Kalley hung up the phone, her doorbell rang. *That never happens,* she thought, perplexed. She mentally reviewed; had she forgotten an appointment or something? She walked to the door but didn't undo the deadbolt.

"Who is it?" Silence. She peered through the peephole. Richard.

CHAPTER 34

Richard's Return

KALLEY SLOWLY OPENED the door with a puzzled look on her face.

"Is that the way you greet me after three years?" Richard held his arms out for Kalley. She ignored him. "I don't feel quite welcome with that greeting."

"What do you expect from me?" she demanded. "A hug and a kiss? Last time I saw you, you were walking out on us with no explanation, so forgive me for not having a welcome home party for you."

He held his arms out slightly, palms up. "Kalley, do we have to go backwards? I'm sorry. I was confused and hurt and I was running out of time with no answers."

"What do you want from me?"

"I want another chance. I want you to forgive me."

"Why should I trust you again?"

"I promise things will be better."

"I don't know about that. I put you before my family and stood by you in our worst times. Did you stick by me? No, you left, thinking—as usual—about nobody but yourself. I worked too hard to get where I am at now, to let you come back and put me in a position where I was before. Never." She closed the door and re-set the bolt.

Richard raised his voice so he could be heard, but it was tinged with tenderness. "I came back to be a father to my son. I'm going to get a job and help out with the finances. I'm ready to be the man you wanted me to be! I can be that now. I need my family. I've changed. You don't have to be bothered with me until I do what I said I'm going to do."

Kalley stood still, listening and thinking. Finally, she called back, "I can't make any promises until I see the new and improved Richard."

"When you do, will you consider taking me back?"

Kalley hedged. "We'll see."

"Is Li'l Rich there?"

Kalley turned, slid the bolt back, and opened the door once more.

"He's at my dad's. They just came back from Lisa's graduation in Virginia. I haven't picked him up yet. Would you like to go with me to pick him up?"

"I just got dropped off, so yeah, I can go with you. Let's ride."

"Let me finish getting dressed and I'll be ready shortly. Have a seat." She grabbed her purse and started down the hall, then stopped and turned around. "How did you find out where I live?"

"My mom told me. She said you've done a wonderful job with our son. Your home is beautiful. You're doing good. I'm proud of you."

Kalley hurried back made straight for the door. "We better go."

She locked the front door and they both got in the car.

Richard asked, "Can I drive?"

"No, we'll have to take it very slow. I can't be rushed."

When they arrived at Keith's cottage, Richard decided to wait outside in the car. As Kalley walked through the front door, Li'l Rich looked outside and saw his mom's car. He ran over to her immediately and hugged her. Kalley picked Li'l Rich up, then headed over to Keith, who was at the window. She gave him a hug and kiss.

"Thank you for loving us the way you do," she said. "We love you back, don't we, Li'l Rich?"

"Yes, we do, Grandpa."

Keith smiled but still seemed preoccupied. He looked at her car again, squinting and putting his hand up to shield the glare.

"Why didn't you invite your new friend in? You didn't have to leave him in the car."

"It's not a new friend, Dad. It's Richard."

"My dad's in the car?" Li'l Rich asked cautiously. "What does he want, Mom?"

"He wants to see you and see how you are doing."

"I thought you said he left us?"

"Oh, he did," Keith affirmed quietly as he gazed at the car. "But now he heard that you got a nice new house and some monthly checks, so of course he came running."

"Dad, it's been three years! Cut him some slack."

"I don't think he'd be nearly this interested if we were all living in the same house right now."

"I haven't told him anything yet," she said.

Keith turned and slowly strode to his favorite chair, then sat down stiffly. "Now there's only two ways this relationship is going to end. I hope and pray that you come to your senses and get fed up with it and end it for good. The other is you'll let him back in your life and it will take something dramatic or life threatening or death, God forbid, for you to see the light, and then you'll end it—if you're not already dead."

"Dad, don't talk like that." She spun around to see her father shielding his face with a handkerchief and pretending to blow his nose.

"Kalley, I love you. There's something wrong, and I can't make you see that. I just know it, and I can't sit here and not tell you. Please make the right choice before it's too late."

"I'll be okay."

"Whatever you do, pray, and I will too. Don't let him come between us. This relationship we have is good."

"I promise, Dad." She gave him a hug, then Li'l Rich and Kalley headed to the door.

⇥⟥◉ ◉⟤⇤

Richard made himself useful all the time. Kalley hadn't let him move in, but he spent most of his time at her house. Kalley would drop Richard off at his mother's house before she put Li'l Rich to bed.

During the day, Richard would stay at the house with Li'l Rich when he wasn't in school. He would watch him while Kalley was at work or at class. He helped Li'l Rich with his homework. Richard was so involved with his son that Kalley would let him drop her off where ever she had to go so he and Li'l Rich could spend more time together. Often, they'd go play basketball and hang out.

Richard would occasionally stay the weekend with Kalley and Li'l Rich. A few months later, Richard's mother got him a job at Yale New Haven Hospital. A few weeks after that, he moved in.

Kalley had conditions for Richard's staying, though. She wrote out a contract and she spelled out her demands. "First, on weekdays, no coming home later than 11:00 p.m. unless it's work-related. Secondly, there will be no drugs or smoking in my house at all. Third, if Li'l Rich isn't around, you can drink beer."

She laid out a financial plan too. Richard was to pay all the bills and Kalley was in charge of the mortgage and food. They would split the cost of things for Li'l Rich. Richard signed the agreement and understood that breaking any of the rules would be cause for immediate eviction.

Finally, Kalley was proud that she had a man who made her life a little easier. She knew he wasn't like her father, but he was trying. He was working hard to support his family and helping her with little things like cooking and grocery shopping and even doing the dishes. He took her out on special occasions like her birthday, and they would have date night or movie night out when there was something good to see.

Kalley and Li'l Rich visited Keith regularly. They took him home cooked meals. If Richard happened to be around at the time, he would drop them off and come back to pick them up when they were ready to leave.

"Where's Richard?" Keith would always ask.

"He dropped us off and will come back to pick us up when I call him," Kalley unfailingly replied.

Keith would look at Kalley. "There's a reason for that. He knows I can see right through him. Give him a little time and he'll be right back to his usual self. You can't teach an old dog new tricks."

One day, Kalley snapped back. "Dad, he's working really hard to save up enough to buy his own car. He takes good care of little Richard, and helps me around the house. He's changed! He even washes dishes."

Keith just sighed. "I hope you're right."

It took Richard another year and a half to purchase his car. It wasn't as nice as his Honda, but it was his and he'd earned it.

During his food delivery rounds at Yale New Haven, Richard heard the nurses' scuttlebutt about a spate of overdose patients from The Catwalk, a strip club three miles from the house.

Richard tried to ignore his instincts, but the inner hustler wouldn't shut up. Every day, Richard would agonize about leaving perfectly green money in other people's pockets when it could be his. In one good night at the club, he could make what he made at the hospital in a week.

Two weeks later, Richard bought his first stash.

That night, Richard told Kalley about his plan. "I can make more selling this on the weekend than I do all week at my job." He explained to Kalley. "I'm not going to do it long term. Just until I bank some money for my family, so I'm taking care of you. I'm the man in this house."

Kalley's face became the mask. She walked back into the bedroom, leaving Richard standing in the kitchen. He had kept his promises to work full time and not bring anything illegal into the house. The extra money would be nice, she thought. Kalley also remembered the discussion she'd had with her dad and knew what he would say.

Whether or not Kalley wanted to admit it, habits travel in packs. It took a few months for Richard to give up the little things he used to do with her on the weekends. Then Li'l Rich noticed his dad wasn't taking him out as much. He would ask, "Dad, are we going to the court this weekend?"

"No, son I'll take you next week. I've got some meetings this afternoon. Next weekend, for sure," Richard would say.

"That's what you said last week," Li'l Rich would complain. "You said the same thing about the game on Thursday."

"Okay, come on. We'll play a quick game of basketball before I go." And that's what it always was: a few quick hoops in the driveway, but no trips or long outings.

Kalley confronted Richard about it one night. "Something is wrong that you don't have time for us anymore. You said your working on Saturday and Sunday would not interfere with your family life. You said it was to bank money for your family and it was just temporary."

"You weren't worried about it when I brought the two flat screen TV's. I didn't hear you fussing when I brought you jewelry and new clothes in the house for you and Li'l Rich."

"Honey, I know you brought us some beautiful things. Of course, I love them. Li'l Rich loves his stuff as well. But they're things, Richard. That's not the same as spending time with us. You're gone all the time now. And we love you, not things. Even during the week, you get up and leave in the middle of the night. You oversleep in the morning and you're late for work. How long do you think you can keep a job like that?"

"You worry too much."

"I must have been crazy to co-sign a loan for a fifty-three thousand dollar Cadillac truck. If you get fired, how do you plan to pay for it?"

"I got this. Don't worry."

Richard took little Richard to the park to play a quick game. He brought him back within thirty minutes, then drove off toward the club.

At the club, Richard had formed a partnership with Sonya, one of the veteran dancers. She lived upstairs. She and the other ladies hardly paid any rent for their apartments, as long as they danced every evening.

When Richard was at work during the week, Sonya would handle his product. She collected and held onto the money. When it sold out, she would page him. At first, he'd picked up the money and brought back a new stash all in the same night. Sonya leaned in close to him and whispered in his ear. That night, she and one of her next-door neighbors gave Richard his first ménage-a-trois. It didn't take long for them to teach Richard which toys and drugs were the most fun to use together.

Kalley sat up in bed one night, watching the taillights of the Escalade recede down the street, and shook her head. How many times did this happen? More nights than not, Richard's phone would buzz, and he'd be ready like a Navy Seal, suddenly silently slipping out the door and getting into the truck.

The money kept coming, though, so Kalley held her peace on the issue. Richard, on the other hand, was calling in sick to Yale New Haven more and more. When he did go in for his shifts, he'd arrive late. The foodservice manager gave him numerous warnings but finally fired him.

Richard felt relieved. Since he was fired, he could at least claim it wasn't his fault. And, better yet, the free time would allow him to ramp up his hustle.

When he arrived home, he carried a newspaper under his arm. He sat down at the table sullenly and flipped to the want ads with a scowl.

"I got fired today," he said from behind the newspaper.

"Well, what did you think? You were always late. You left early. You called in sick with every illness known to man and some that even the hospital hadn't heard of."

Richard put the paper down.

"Baby, wait a minute. It wasn't my fault."

"We have an agreement; you signed it."

"I'll find another job real quick. I've got a couple of interviews lined up. It won't take long to find another. I'll go make some more phone calls."

He walked into the family room where he could have some privacy. He dialed the club. He spoke softly into the phone. "I'll see you in the next hour," he whispered.

Richard had made up his mind. *No more jobs for me,* he thought.

CHAPTER 35

Richard's Deceit

FOR KALLEY'S SAKE, Richard picked up the newspaper every day and pretended to look for work.

"Did you get the job?" Kalley would ask every day.

Richard had to remember to hang his head and look sad. "Naw, Babe. I went to the other hospitals and the restaurant where you used to work. They're not hiring right now. Something will come through."

Late one night, Richard met Sonya in her apartment as usual. She reached for the light switch, but Richard grabbed her hand. "Not tonight," he said with a smile. "You want to make more money?"

Sonya chuckled. "That's my middle name: money. What's up?"

"Well, you know I did a bid for dealing?"

"I knew you were in the joint."

"Well, I didn't sell anybody out, so I believe I can go back to my New York connect."

"So why are you telling me?"

"I am going to get in touch with my connect. I got busted the last time I went to New York alone so I want to have someone with me. I also want to go by train this time. No more car for me. If you carry the work, it'll be safer. They won't be as quick to check a woman. Now, I think I can get a half a key on credit, which would turn twenty to thirty thousand. The only problem is where we can hide the shit."

"I could stash it."

"Where?"

Sonya got up and walked over to her bed, which was in a corner. "Help me pull out this bed." They both pulled the bed out, then pulled up the carpet. There was a little wooden hatch in the floor. She lifted up two panels, revealing a long holding area lined with plastic.

"But this would be the first place they will look if we sell it here. We can put it here, and sell it from one of your girlfriends' rooms. When she sells out, you can restock her, and she can pay you. She can keep a little for herself."

Sonya nodded. Richard continued. "We can go 24/7 and go from part-time to full-time in no time. I'll give you a percentage off each bundle. We can use one of your girls to also help bag it up. Each half should flip in three to four weeks, max."

"Well, let's get on it." They both smiled and Richard flipped the lightswitch.

⇀╼◉ ◉╾↼

The train trip went smoothly. They took an off-peak Metro North train into Manhattan. They went out for lunch, then did a little shopping. Afterward, they took the subway up to a brownstone in the north Bronx.

Two of Richard's friends, T-Bone and Mad Dog, were there. They were glad to see him since he hadn't snitched, so they got right down to business. The deal was they were going to give Richard a half a key on consignment. The cost was thirteen thousand dollars; however, they wanted fifteen thousand back at a thousand dollars every two weeks until it was paid in full. That was their favor to him to get back on his feet since he had brought them so much business from Connecticut in the past. They joked and laughed like old times for a while, and then Sonya loaded up her bags and Richard shook hands with T-Bone and Mad Dog. "Ey," T-Bone said, scanning the block and texting his spotters, "Silence is golden." Sonya and Richard nodded.

They were back in New Haven by 10 p.m. As soon as they got off the train, they went their separate ways like strangers. Sonya hailed a cab and Richard walked four blocks over to where he'd parked his truck. They'd already arranged to meet at Sonya's apartment at 2 a.m., after the club closed.

At home, Richard played with Li'l Rich and teased Kalley playfully. *It's all worth it,* he thought to himself. *Hustling is equal opportunity.*

At midnight, Richard decided to go to the club and make sure Sonya had everything in order. When he got to the club, he didn't see Sonya.

He asked her friend, Cinnamon, "Where's Sonya?"

"Oh, she moved back home. She had been planning to go for some time to help her mother out with her daughter. She left this morning."

"What!?" Richard couldn't believe it. His heart started pounding, and he felt the hair stand up on the back of his neck.

Richard bolted up the stairs to Sonya's apartment. He banged on the door, calling, "Sonya! I know you're in there."

Other girls that were in their rooms came out in the hallway. "Sonya moved out," they told him.

"Sonya!" Richard practically screamed.

"She's gone back home to Maryland. Didn't you drop her off?"

"What the fuck?" That's when Richard lost it. He began kicking and kicking her door until he broke it down. Then he ran inside to see all her belongings were gone. Frantically, he flipped over the bed, pulled up the carpet, then the panels. The spot was just as empty as it had been when she'd showed it to him not even a week earlier.

The two large, muscled bouncers jumped on Richard, restrained him and threw him down the stairs.

"Look," the owner, Mark, said, "Sonya doesn't work here anymore. If you come back again, you might not be so lucky. Stay away from here."

CHAPTER 36

Chickens Come Home To Roost

KALLEY WAS WAITING for Richard when he walked back into the house. "What happened to you, Richard?! I knew something like this would happen. Just knew it!" Kalley scream-whispered as she paced the kitchen.

Richard told Kalley about his trip to New York and how he'd gone to check on his distributor, only to discover she'd left. She lit into him all the more. "How the hell do you think you are going to pay the Dominicans? You know they don't play about their money. You have really fucked up!" She began to pace the floor again. "They could come here and kill me and our son. What were you thinking?"

She stopped by the refrigerator. "My father was right about you. You haven't changed. You are pulling me and Li'l Rich down."

Richard got up. "I'm'a make it right," he grunted as he grabbed his keys and walked out.

He knew he only had one week to come up with the Dominicans' money. He pawned the two flat screen TVs the next day while Kalley was at work. He got three thousand, which was about as well as he could hope to do on such short notice.

Out of the money, he paid eight hundred for his truck and car insurance and five ninety-nine for his bills, which left him with about sixteen hundred. He debated the basic choice: pay Mad Dog and T-Bone one thousand, and only have six hundred left. Or he could buy sixteen hundred dollars' worth of product and be a little late with the first payment.

Richard drove to a crack house where one of Li'l Red's homeboys worked. He bought two and a half ounces with the sixteen hundred dollars. "Ha," Richard said softly as he inspected the goods. "Cheap and quick to flip."

Richard knew he had a good thing at the club, and it wouldn't take long to get rid of his product and turn a profit, provided he could apologize to Mark.

As he pulled into The Catwalk's parking lot, three men in sunglasses with automatic guns got out of a car and surrounded the truck.

"You're not too bright," said the biggest one through the driver's side window. The one outside the passenger window flipped his gun and smashed the window out with the butt. He rummaged through the glove box until he found the registration card while Richard watched helplessly. "Now stay away from this spot or you're gonna be one dead nigga."

Richard wiped sweat from his forehead as he drove toward the projects, his old home turf.

→▬ ▬←

Richard set up shop down at the foot of the hill, just far away enough to feel comfortable. He could see the top of the high-rise building where a young gang sold weed and pills. He hoped there wouldn't be any conflict. Things were moving pretty slow, but there were some reliable customers and a lot of old friends came around and showed him love. Everyone seemed really happy to see him. It felt good to set up shop in the neighborhood where he'd grown up.

As soon as the sun went down darkness started to settle over the neighborhood, everything became eerily quiet. Richard's gut told him to call it quits for the night. But if he left then, when would it be the right time to come back? "I know this hood," he said to nobody. "I'm just jumpy is all."

Richard took out his phone and sat down. Suddenly, about eight young boys surrounded him.

One of them pistol whipped Richard across the temple from the back; Rich gasped and curled up on the floor. Then someone shot out the window and into his car. When Richard's eyes cleared, he looked up as his chest tightened. He hadn't seen Little Red at all since doing time.

"Yo, Red—"

"Don't 'yo Red' me like we still boys or nothin' like that," Red snapped, leaning over toward Richard. "Run yo' ass back to the 'burbs. They held you down this long; let 'em hold you down some more. 'Cause in my hood? Now? You just a dumb muhfucka tryin'a creep on Red's turf. Get the fuck outta here with your prettyboy truck. I got half a mind to end you right now 'cause back in the day don't pay today.

Richard jumped in his truck and sped off, panicking, thinking how he almost got shot in the face. Since he'd made a few sales, he stopped at a corner store and bought a pack of cigarettes to try to calm his nerves.

When he got in the door, Kalley and Little Richard were just getting in.

"Hey, Dad? How was your day?" Little Richard asked.

Richard didn't even answer. He just tore downstairs to the basement.

"What's wrong with Dad?"

"He's probably had a hard day, but he'll be all right. Just go to bed. Love you, son." Kalley gave her son a hug and a kiss on his cheek.

She was about to go downstairs when she noticed the answering machine's beep and saw the number five glowing on the screen. When she pressed the "play" button, four of them were for Richard. T-Bone and Mad Dog wanted to know why they hadn't heard from Richard, and why he wasn't answering his pages. Each one ended with a more exasperated rendition of the same line: "Please contact us as soon as you get the message."

With that, Kalley went into the basement. She couldn't believe how disheveled and bruised Richard looked.

"You look a mess. You've got Li'l Rich worried sick about you. And then there's me, but when has that mattered..." she trailed off. She began to pace the basement floor. "You're not spending any time here. This reminds me of how you were before you went to jail. In fact, you are in that same predicament. What happened to the money from the TVs? Why couldn't you pay them to keep them off your back?" She paused. "You know what? I don't even want to know. But I can tell you this. If they come to my house, I am going to call the police and have them locked up." She light-stepped up the stairs, closed the door noiselessly, and then tiptoed to the bedroom and cried into her pillow.

As Kalley tried to cry her troubles away, Richard tried to smoke his away. They both woke in the morning, empty and confused.

CHAPTER 37

Kalley, The Enabler

THE NEXT DAY when Kalley got home after work, she saw the iconic outline of a Lincoln Town Car parked across the street at the corner. She saw reflections of passing cars mirrored in the tinted windows, then disappear.

She opened the door and called for Richard.

She finally located him in the basement sleeping on the cot. His pager was vibrating like crazy. It was sitting against the wall, so every time it buzzed she could hear it upstairs. She walked over and picked up the pager. The screen showed the same number from the answering machine's caller ID. She tossed it back onto the floor, stepping around cigarette butts, ashes, and beer bottles that littered the floor.

"Wake up, Richard," she said, shaking him.

"What? What?" Richard's eyes bulged and darted back and forth.

"Richard, I think the guys from New York are up at the corner waiting for you to see if they could catch you leaving or coming. Now you straighten this out because I am not going to have them watching my house."

"Kalley, quiet down," Richard said, hushing her. "How do you know it is them? They don't know where we live."

"Yes, they do. My phone number is listed and so is my address. If it ain't them, you go out and look. I'm going to get Li'l Rich from the babysitter. In case they're waiting for me to bring Li'l Rich home, I'm not coming home tonight because it is not safe here. Text me when it's okay to come back, and if I don't hear from you by tomorrow night, I'm gonna let the cops sort it all out."

Kalley tried to keep her composure as she walked to her car. She pulled down the sun visor and checked her makeup in the mirror. It had been such an empty threat. What were the police going to do? Tell the Dominicans to go back to New York every single time they showed up? To park in the driveway after midnight? Before she went to pick up little Richard, she stopped at the ATM and got some cash.

Kalley hemmed and hawed about what to do as she drove to the babysitter's house. When she got there, she paid the sitter to keep Li'l Rich overnight and promised it wouldn't happen again.

She drove back home, past the same black Town Car parked in the same place. She walked into the house and wondered if Richard was even there. No lights were on, and only the hum of the refrigerator cut the silence. She turned on the basement light at the top of the stairs and padded down the wooden steps slowly.

She found Richard huddled in the laundry room between the washing machine and dryer. He dripped sweat. His eyes bulged preternaturally, and Kalley smelled an odor that was cigarettes or weed coming from a smoldering joint on the floor.

She looked at him for a long time. He looked, but not at her; more through her, out into the darkness of the storage room. "Look," she said, "I am going to try to handle this situation for you, but you have to promise that you are going to get help. You're out of control. You have to go to the Labor Department or even McDonald's or whatever it takes to help me out with the bills. And that doesn't include selling drugs."

Richard didn't even acknowledge her words. She bent and then stooped down so they were face to face. She stifled a sob. They'd snuck peaks at each others' faces in the back of U.S. History class, back when he was intriguing and rakishly rebellious and she was unattainable and charmingly innocent. Hers had not changed that much, she realized, remembering how she applied her makeup every morning with the same strokes she'd learned and used in high school. Richard's face was taut but wrinkled all at once. Hard lines carried sweat to his temples, where rivulets ran down to his tattered white tee shirt. Rivers coursed from his armpits, and the wet mess clung to him.

"I'm high as fuck," Richard slurred.

"I love you, Richard," she hiccupped. "And I always will. Can't do a damn thing about it." She stood up before the tears could overflow her eyes. Richard's eyes did not follow her.

"I'd rather be behind in my bills than to see you, me, or our son dead. I'd rather be behind on my mortgage than have to explain why you were killed to your son. So I am fixing this. I don't know what else to do."

Richard nodded.

Kalley fished out a large manila envelope from deep in a chest in the attic. Richard was bailing them out of this, she told herself as she counted out ten hundred dollar bills from when things had been good. She'd begged for money to buy things for herself but then stashed a little extra, in case something went wrong. She put the bills into her pocket and walked down the street and straight up to the driver's window of the black Town Car.

She tapped on the glass, then took a few steps back, edging back so that she could take evasive action if needed.

The window rolled down, revealing two Dominican men, one light and one dark. "Do you know Richard?" the light one asked.

"Do I have to worry about you shooting me or trying to grab me?" Kalley asked.

"No. If that's what we wanted to do, we could've done it already."

"Follow my car," Kalley told him. "And I gave your license plate number to a friend, so if I don't make it back here she knows what to do."

Kalley drove to the police station and parked. The Town Car paused at the entrance, then slowly pulled in beside her. She got out and approached the Town Car again, this time on the passenger side.

"Sit in my car," she said to the dark one. He followed her to her car and sat in the passenger seat.

She handed him the one thousand dollars, which he counted after licking his thumb.

"What's Richard's arrangement? How much does he owe?" she asked fridigdly.

"Two thousand per month for seven months and one thousand in the last month."

Kalley's brow furrowed and her eyes narrowed. "Fifteen thousand. No wonder you're here."

"It's nothing to kill over," the dark one said with mock comfort.

"I can give you one thousand per month. You can deal with Richard, or you can deal with me."

The dark man pushed his sunglasses up into his dreadlocks. "You are one special lady. Richard mentioned you."

"I'm sure he did," Kalley said evenly. "Do you deal with me or with him?"

"Tell that excuse for a man never to call me again. You can call anytime." He kissed Kalley's hand. "Thank you for not letting this situation get ugly."

The Town Car drove away, and Kalley wiped her hand on the passenger seat so hard that it stung a little.

Kalley drove home on the edge of tears. She had no clue how she would handle the mortgage or the bills. Maybe she could get Lisa to advance her some more of the proceeds from the house. She prayed for the first time in years. "God," Kalley whispered softly. "If you're still paying attention, please… please get Li'l Rich out of this okay. Please save him, even if you don't save me."

CHAPTER 38

The Downward Spiral

KALLEY TOSSED AND turned all night. Sure, she had a part-time position as a clerk at City Hall, but she still didn't make as much as she'd made working overtime at the restaurant. She scoffed gently thinking about it: she only brought home one thousand dollars a month after taxes. The mortgage alone was nine hundred. With her father's check, and when Richard had been helping, things had been doable. Even without Richard's money, things had been possible. But without any help, no kind of math could offer a good answer.

She didn't even go to class after work that day. She wanted to get home and have Li'l Rich call his grandfather to get Aunt Lisa's phone number. After Li'l Rich softened Keith up, Kalley got Lisa's phone number from him. She waited until after seven o'clock that evening to call Lisa, hoping desperately that she'd be home and that the conversation would go well.

When Lisa answered the phone, Kalley got straight to the point. "Lisa, this is Kalley. I'm calling because I need to see if I can get more money allotted to me each month."

"It's not my position to give you more without Daddy saying so," Lisa said calmly.

"Daddy left you in charge because of his disease. What matters to him is that you get your half and I get mine."

"I do things the way I am told," she said with a trace of annoyance. "If you had listened in your time, you wouldn't be in the shape you're in today. So please don't call my home to tell me how to run Daddy's show. You get that straight with Daddy and he will give me the go-ahead."

Kalley hung up without saying goodbye. "Damn," she hissed. She couldn't call Keith and re-negotiate. It had to do with Richard, after all. Dad would just tell her to have him get himself together.

Richard, meanwhile, finally built up enough confidence to go outside. He worked on a per diem basis for whoever would pay cash, so he mowed a lot of lawns and cleaned a lot of gutters. He didn't make a lot doing it, either, but he made more than he told Kalley about. Every night he bought a few bags, which he smoked up right away.

It took a year, but the foreclosure finally happened. Kalley cried as she packed up their few possessions. She and a few neighbors loaded the U-Haul truck, and she and Li'l Rich drove everything over to Church Street South, the only place with an apartment they could realistically afford.

Li'l Rich was not quite as little as he was before. The almost-five-ten twelve year old transferred into Troup Middle School, where he quickly learned how to get by with the minimum effort. Every day he felt more distant from Richard, whom he almost never saw, and Kalley, who had plenty of worries before thinking about Li'l Rich.

He skipped school once or twice and went to find what he could find. He knew not to get mixed up in anything involving crack, so he steered clear of gangs, dealers, and users. Plus, he didn't want to run into his dad. Eventually, Li'l Rich developed a network of other people whose hearts were equally homeless. While none of them would necessarily call the others friends, they often walked to Connecticut Post Mall or, when the weather was bad, stayed at each others' houses and apartments whenever their parents were at work.

Of course, his grades plummeted. The school referred his name to the local truancy officer, who stopped by to meet Kalley and set up an appointment for a hearing. "I mean, he needs to understand the situation. He's on academic probation for the next year, no matter what. And," the officer added, "if things got worse, that'll probably get him a case in the juvenile justice system."

It wasn't even basketball season before Li'l Rich's academic skid made him ineligible to try out for the team. He tried to act nonchalant, but it broke his heart. That's where he'd felt best for years: on the court and on the field. He pined for it and tried to stay away from places and people that reminded him of what he no longer had.

Kalley tried to talk to him. "What's happening with your grades? You used to get A's without even really trying! Please don't throw your life away. You're young. You can get back on track."

Li'l Rich, the spitting image of his father, just could not abide school if he couldn't participate in athletics. He started to hang out in coffeeshops in West Rock when the weather turned cold, and he met a lot of college students and artists. His old days of doodling in class turned into days of designing tattoos for local artists and working on graphic novels he wasn't even old enough to legally sell. He sold them anyway, which got him into parties at Southern Connecticut State. That's where he had his first cigarette, his first beer, his first joint, and his first girlfriend.

Kalley didn't have time to put in the detective work necessary for keeping up with Li'l Rich, but she didn't have to. When the police broke up a raucous spring break party in West Haven, Li'l Rich was booked for underage drinking, violating curfew, and resisting arrest. The judge told Li'l Rich he needed to stay off the radar, go back to school, and avoid Juvenile Hall.

Desperate, Kalley didn't want to see her young son locked up. It was so odd—he wasn't lost, but he was acting a solid eight years older than his age. She did something she didn't want to do, but she felt this was the best choice.

"Li'l Rich," she said as they pulled into the parking lot after the court hearing, "Call your Aunt Lisa and see if she will let you stay with her."

"Aunt Lisa," he said when she picked up. "It's Rich. I have a special favor to ask. Could I come stay with you for a while? I have to get a fresh start—new school, new friends, new plan. You're successful and I want to be successful too." He was surprised at how much he believed the words coming out of his mouth. He hadn't planned on saying any of that.

"Did you call me on your own or did your mom get you to call?" Lisa asked. The reverie shattered. "My mom said I had to call, but I think it's a good idea." After ten seconds of silence, Li'l Rich handed the phone to Kalley. "She stopped talking," he said.

Lisa's mind tried to process everything. She was still learning her job. She worked almost twenty-five hours of overtime every week. She thought about how her parents had bent over backwards helping Kalley, and how it had just enabled her to stay with Richard. She thought about how Kalley had gotten on her feet and then let Richard back into her life. She thought about Kalley struggling just to keep them in their shabby apartment.

Kalley reluctantly took the phone.

"Li'l Rich has both of his parents there to help," Lisa said brusquely. "Stop trying to take the easy way out by sending him to me. If you'd paid attention to your son, you wouldn't have needed to call me. You know what the problem is. He is crying out for help, but you are too busy trying to raise a grown man to realize what your son is trying to say to you. I'm not cleaning up your messes like Mama and Daddy did. Nobody can keep giving when there's no such thing as enough."

"Thanks for your speech. Look, I didn't call for a lecture; I called for help. It would have been far more foolish for me to tell myself that things would just start to go better on their own. But that's all right. I almost forgot! I called the queen of things going perfectly. Maybe she doesn't know a whole bunch about what needs to happen when things go wrong." With that, hung up and tossed the phone onto the couch. Still, though, she had to admit she wasn't surprised.

→⊨⊙ ⊙⊨←

"Uh, Mr. McCall?" Jessica said, looking up into the gaunt, tired-looking face of a man she thought must have been far too old to be Richie's father. "Is Richie's dad around?"

Richard stood stock still, staring vacantly at Jessica.

"I'm Jessica, Richie's friend," she said. "We were bringing a keg to a party and we got pulled over. Richie took the rap for me because they found some weed in my trunk, and he claimed he put it there before he picked me up."

Richard nodded his head, trying to show concern. It never crossed his mind to ask why Li'l Rich had been driving, and whose car it had really been, and where he'd gotten the money for the party favors. Or why he hadn't been in school.

Richard's aimless gaze unnerved Jessica. "Uh, okay, have a nice day..." she said, walking away as quickly as she could without running.

→⊨⊙ ⊙⊨←

Kalley worked overtime whenever she could—it wasn't often that the city approved it, so when it came around, she gobbled up the opportunity. At nine thirty that night, she kicked her heels off and opened the fridge, grabbed a yogurt, and flopped down on the couch.

Richard zombie-walked past her, vaguely stammering. "L-l-l-Li'l Rich got locked up. Locked him up for n-nothing, they did." Kalley dropped the yogurt, ran out the door, ran back in, grabbed her shoes and put them on hastily, and scampered back out the door. At the precinct, the duty officer told her Li'l Rich could not be released and had to go before the judge within seventy-two hours.

Kalley went back home and cried on and off all night. The yogurt stain never came out of the couch.

In the morning, she called Lisa. To avoid the brutal capital area traffic, Lisa had already left for work. The message machine picked up. "Hi, you've reached Lisa Davidson. Please leave—" Kalley pressed the pound key furiously and the machine beeped.

"Well, Lisa Davidson, Richard McCall Junior is now a ward of the juvenile detention center. I have tried my level best at every point, in every situation, but ain't nothing changed. I'm glad I busted you upside your head. It wasn't enough that you let Mommy die, then you wouldn't take my son before the system could get to him. You could have saved my house, but you weren't about to do that, either. I'm glad it's all perfect with you, your career, and Daddy. As long as we are alive, you won't ever have to worry about me and my son. From this day forward, we are not, nor are we to be known as, family. Blood honors blood, but you just look on as if none of this has anything to do with you. Goodbye, Lisa Davidson."

⤜●═⬝

Lisa sighed as she listened to the message late that night. She poured herself a glass of moscato and reflected back on everything. She should have been sadder, she told herself, and yet she wasn't. "Serves her right," she said dismissively. It felt good to say it. Betty had always said, "Turnabout is fair play," and finally Kalley could feel what it was like to suffer and not be recognized for years on end. "Better get you on down to church," she quipped. "God might help you, but I ain't the one." She grabbed the remote and turned the television on.

CHAPTER 39

Juvenile Court

AT COURT, KALLEY tried everything to talk to the state's attorney, the social worker, the arresting officer, or anybody else. She had to get clemency for Li'l Rich—which pretty much meant home arrest—and if they would only listen… but the presiding Honorable Judge Martha Halloran thought differently.

Judge Halloran peered over her eyeglasses as she looked up from the case in front of her. "I have read all the material that's been gathering in Rich McCall's file over the past year. He has been warned. But he is incorrigible. He doesn't take school seriously. When he was caught driving a stolen car without a license to transport beer and marijuana, no one came to see about him until after ten o'clock that night. I have to set an example for him and hope that this will save him from further incarceration later in life. Richard McCall, Jr., you are hereby remanded to two years in Juvenile camp. You will see me again, Lord willing, at the end of that time."

Kalley broke down crying. The social worker had to walk her out of the courtroom and calm her down. After she calmed down, Kalley resolved that she would work hard to get out of the environment she was living in so that Li'l Rich would have a chance to survive.

⋆⟜◉ ◉⊸⋆

That evening around eight-thirty, Richard stepped out of Kaiser Whitney Staffing on Elm Street with his daily pay of eighty-nine dollars in his pocket. Before going home, he went to the spot and bought three bags. He stopped at People's Choice to get a pack of cigarettes and then went home. He mumbled as he walked. "Used'a be a bag could rev me all night, just put a sprinkle on and whooooo… well, the coke been changing up on me now. Really need three bags, but I gotta stretch the two."

As soon as he opened the door, Kalley took one look at him and immediately flashed back to the night she'd found him huddled between the washer and the dryer.

"Richard, you have a problem," she said sadly. "Go get help. Now."

Richard tried to whip out his charming smile, but it came out as a crocodile grin. "Babe, spot me a twenty—"

Kalley's rage erupted as she screamed louder than she ever remembered herself screaming in her life. "Richard, I dropped you off at work this morning. Where is your check?"

"I been, well, out at the track, an'—"

"Bullshit!" Kalley felt herself go faint and retreated to the couch.

"Kalley, could you please lend me twenty dollars and I'll give it back to you tomorrow?"

Kalley yelled at the top of her voice, "Where is it? Where is your check?!"

Richard began to hyperventilate and twitch. "I'll go tomorrow for help, but if I don't get a taste tonight, I will go out into the street and risk my life. I am desperate. I don't care what I have to do."

Kalley could see the hunger in his eyes. She wanted to help him, but she was out of money. She shook her head.

"Listen, Babe, I know how I can get right tonight and then tomorrow I'll go to the clinic. Right when they open. C'mere," he said, waving her to his side. "Lemme explain."

A neighborhood gang used a mailbox in Kalley's apartment building hallway as a drop spot. To anyone who didn't know, the mailbox appeared to be locked.

"All you have to do is stick your fingers up under the box and it opens up," Richard said. Before Kalley got the drugs, Richard was to call the police to chase the young boys away for a little while.

Everything worked like a charm. Kalley brought the drugs back to Richard. What they hadn't counted on, though, was a boy who made trips to the corner store for the dealers. He lived across the hall from the mailboxes and had been watching through his peephole the whole time. As soon as Kalley left with the drugs, the boy told the dealers everything once they returned.

By the time Richard had smoked the fifth pack, there was a knock at the door. Richard looked through the peephole and knew he had to feign innocence. Before he could open the door, four men kicked in the door and stormed the apartment. One grabbed him by the collar.

"I don't know what you're talking about," Richard said, slurring a little. His eyes darted from place to place and didn't stop.

"You a lie, nigga. We can see the bags here on the table."

Richard pointed to the hallway. "She's back there, sleeping," he said.

The guys slapped Richard up but let him out the door. Then they went into the back room and yanked Kalley out of the bed. They beat her and stomped her head, her face, her stomach, and anything else that was visible. She had woken up long enough just to cry, "What's going on?" when a boot to the face knocked her unconscious. They left her body, bloody and crumpled, at the side of the bed.

CHAPTER 40

Ralph Comes Back

RICHARD RAN MANY blocks without looking back, even though he felt someone chasing him. When he finally came down from his high, he was exhausted but found a payphone and called the police anonymously. He walked the streets doggedly, hoping he could find someone or some way to get high again.

Back at the apartment, several officers searched for information to notify Kalley's next of kin. They found her driver's license and insurance card in her wallet, which had a small piece of paper tucked behind it. Lisa had sent Kalley their father's information when Keith first arrived at the retirement community.

When the officers contacted the retirement residence, they were told that Keith's Alzheimer's has progressed so rapidly that he could be of no help to them. The officers asked about the mother and other women in the photo. Mrs. Little, the administrative assistant said, "The mother is deceased and the sister left direct orders that she isn't to be contacted for any reason other than issues concerning her father."

The police looked through the wallet's contents again. They found several family photos, one of which had a handwritten note and phone number on the bottom, "Call granddad—anytime. 843-777-4272." The officers called the number at the bottom of the picture.

Ralph answered on the first ring. When the officers explained to Ralph what had happened to Kalley, his first question was, "Why are you contacting me? Why didn't you call her father or sister?" He'd heard about Carol's death, and was surprised that her father, Keith, and sister were not their first point of contact.

178

After they explained Keith's condition and Lisa's estrangement from Kalley, Ralph paused for a moment. "Okay, I'll be there on the next plane I can get out on," he said simply. "What hospital is she in?"

Ralph took a flight out that same night, arriving at the hospital before daybreak the next morning. He didn't bother checking into the hotel to drop off his luggage first. He wanted to be at Kalley's side as soon as he could. Hurrying through the hospital halls, he cantered brokenly down the hallway. His cane clacked and his feet shuffled as fast as they could.

When he found the room, Ralph was taken aback at how bruised and purple Kalley was. Her eyes were swollen shut. He was surprised she was even alive. She was on oxygen.

"Dear, poor girl," Ralph said, tears smarting his eyes.

Then he pulled himself together, and thought about it. Ralph did everything possible to make Kalley comfortable, watching closely as her chest rose and fell with each faint breath. That night she developed a high fever, which made her condition that much more complicated. Ralph slept in a chair in her room and decided to stay until she was out of danger. He woke every few hours to check on her.

As the hours went by, the fever went down. Ralph got a hotel room the next day but still spent most of his time at the ICU.

As the days passed, Ralph decided to talk to Kalley, even though she hadn't come out of the coma. He'd read an article in which neurologists claimed that comatose patients could hear but not respond to everything going on around them. Ralph told Kalley stories about her mother, Carol, proudly sharing how smart Carol had been when she was young. As the hours passed, Ralph hoped for improvement. Kalley stayed stable.

"I came and saw you when you were a little girl. You and your sister were so cute. I came there to recover after your mother had given me a kidney and saved my life. I feel so bad that she's gone and I'm still here. I owe your mother my life. I'll stay here, Kalley. Don't worry. Take your time, and we'll get through this together."

Ralph ate his dinner in Kalley's room, instead of the cafeteria where most family members went for the occasional reprieve. After eating his meal, he read Bible verses to end their day together. This became the routine.

About a week later, Kalley's time in the hospital needed to be reassessed. The specialist asked to meet with Ralph. They discussed her condition, which was improving. They let him know how important it was for him to spend as much time as possible with Kalley during this vital time. "It is important that she sees a familiar face when she comes to."

Ralph was happy about what the doctor was saying; however, he began to question whether his presence would actually help Kalley's recovery. Would she remember him? They had only spoken on the phone a few times within the past year. Their only time spent together was when Carol brought him to her house to recover after surgery. They called each other on their birthdays and sent holiday cards, but it had been a distant relationship.

That night after dinner, Ralph selected special passages to read to Kalley. They all centered on forgiveness, strength, and mercy. When he got back to his hotel room, he didn't bother turning on the lights. He got down on his knees and began to pray.

"God, I never question your work or your decisions, but right now, I am so confused. I want to help Kalley in any way I can, for Carol's sake and for her family. Through your love, Carol gave me a new life. Am I doing more harm than good? Kalley needs a familiar face. Oh, Lord, speak to me. Help me understand."

Ralph sighed and asked for revelation for half an hour, but then he started to get dizzy and he pulled himself up onto the bed. Soon, he lay down and fell asleep fully clothed.

CHAPTER 41

Ralph's Redemption

THE NEXT MORNING, Ralph contacted Officer Mendez, who had originally called him when the incident happened. So far, the police had not found the perpetrators.

"You know the sister had left instructions not to contact her regarding Kalley, but I can give you the father's residential information."

"Okay," Ralph said.

Address in hand, Ralph took a cab to the gated community. He took a deep breath and smiled as he asked the receptionist if Keith Davidson was awake and able to have visitors.

Ralph was asked to sign in, then given a brief orientation about the facility and the rules and regulations. A nurse escorted him to Keith's unit. "He used to have a cottage," she said, "But he's been struggling more recently. We brought him down here last week. Sadly, he thinks he's still in the cottage."

Keith had lost weight since Ralph last seen him. He looked feeble, just a shadow of the muscular man he'd once been. His hair was gray and his speech was garbled. He had a TV on, and was watching "Ladder 49."

"He loves this one," his nurse explained. "Good thing it's on demand, because he really does demand it."

Ralph smiled wryly. "Yes, he used to be a fireman."

"Well, that's one thing he remembers for sure."

The nurse left and Ralph walked over and stood by Keith's side.

"Keith, do you remember me? I'm Ralph. Carol's stepfather. Remember I stayed with you and your family?"

Keith's eyes glazed over.

After twenty minutes, Ralph realized it didn't matter whether Keith was having a good day or a bad day. The staff had warned Ralph about the severity of Keith's condition, and Ralph realized he'd been holding out foolish hope.

"I'd, ummm, better get ready," Keith said slowly. "My son's wedding is coming up. And... and Carol will be home to cook dinner soon."

Ralph's eyes started to fill. "That's wonderful," he said. "Congratulate him for me."

"Are you staying for dinner?" Keith asked in what seemed like a moment of lucidity.

"No, I'm going to get ready to get going. It was good seeing you," Ralph said, standing up from his chair as a knock came at the door.

"That must be my wife," Keith said.

It was the nurse, coming to give Keith his meds. She appeared to be in her late fifties. After she gave Keith his meds, she turned and introduced herself. "Hi, my name is Zaire Baker." Then her face broke into wrinkles of genuine concern. "How is your granddaughter doing?"

"Kalley is in a coma, and there has been no change in her condition."

"That's just evil, what those people did to her. It was in the paper. I remember the few times she came to visit her father, and she was always a respectful and pleasant young woman. I wish there was something I could do."

Ralph hesitated, but then ventured, "Well, maybe you can help. Kalley needs her sister. I know what the staff said about Lisa's request, but can you give me Lisa's address and phone number?"

"I'm sorry," Nurse Baker heaved. "I can't disclose that information. Lisa's request is that we don't give out her information, and if we go against her wishes, she could sue us. Or worse, we could get shut down. I'll tell you what. When she calls to speak to her father, we'll advise her of the severity of her sister's condition."

Just before Nurse Baker stepped out the room, she turned to Ralph. "Can you please stay just a little bit longer? Why don't you read a few pages of Keith's diary to him? When he first came here, he spent quite a bit of time writing about his family."

Ralph was hesitant at first. Then he thought of Kalley, lying helpless in bed, at the mercy of God. He went back to where Keith sat. "Can I see your stories you wrote, Keith?" he asked.

Keith seemed pleased to share his diary. He went and found a notebook that was in his dresser drawer. He handed the notebook over to Ralph without questioning him.

Ralph skipped around and read lines from the journal to himself. His hand slipped and the journal's pages surged past, revealing the interior of the back cover. There, in shaky but legible handwriting, were Lisa's phone number and address.

Ralph smiled and released a breath. A large load had been lifted from his shoulders. "Thank you, God."

⇥▶ ◀⇤

Ralph took a cab back to the hotel. At first, he thought he would call Lisa, but he remembered the strict instructions she'd left not to contact her regarding Kalley. He wondered what could have come between the two sisters because they had been as close as two peas in a pod when they were little. He remembered how they would fall asleep with their arms wrapped around each other during their afternoon naps.

He rethought his plan. Lisa would probably be furious with him for meddling in family business. But he had to have faith and help Lisa focus on Kalley. Lisa didn't know what had happened, and she needed to. Ralph booked the next flight out to Washington, D.C.

⇥▶ ◀⇤

The cab pulled up in front of a six-year old colonial, perched on a well-manicured lawn. Ralph walked up to the perfectly bricked pathway to the large oak front door.

The doorbell was the Westminster Chimes, a falling *dong-dong-dong-dong* followed by a rising *dong-dong-dong-dong.*

Ralph knocked twice. He heard Lisa call out from inside. "Who is it?"

"It's Ralph," he called out. "I stayed with you guys when y'all were younger. You might not remember."

Lisa peeked through the door hole, then slowly opened the front door and let Ralph in. She looked at him.

"I kind of remember you from family pictures. How did you get my address?"

"Can I just come in for a few minutes and explain?"

"Don't waste your time," Lisa said. "A reporter from the *Register* called me and told me about Kalley. I'm sorry you've come this far, but my sister's—well, the woman who said that we could no longer be family, her business is none of mine."

"I don't know what happened between you and your sister, but this is bigger. She's your sister, no matter what she says—you know she's a stubborn one—and she is in a bad position and she needs you. The doctor says she has to see a familiar face when she comes out of the coma."

"She can see her boyfriend when she comes out of the coma."

"No, she can't. Not him, not anyone has been there for her since I arrived."

Lisa didn't say anything.

Ralph went on. "I know your mother would not accept your attitude in this situation. She would never leave you without knowing you are going to be at your sister's side. And whatever you happen to feel about it, I know one thing: I owe this to your mother."

He could see Lisa's growing anger. "You don't owe my family anything. Anyhow, why are you so involved in this mess, for that matter? You don't really know us. If you were that concerned about my mother, then why didn't you bother to come to her funeral?"

"Look, I don't have an argument for what you are feeling or saying. I got issues that I'm still working on, but I'm not the same person I was then. I'm not trying to come in and act like I had a relationship with you or Kalley."

"Then why?"

"I would walk to hell and back for Carol if she asked me to. If it wasn't for her, I wouldn't even be standing here in your home."

Lisa had a baffled look on her face. "What do you mean, you wouldn't be here?"

Ralph paused for a second. "She saved my life. I was on my deathbed. I needed a kidney donor."

Before he could finish his sentence, Lisa exploded. "Wait a minute! You're the one who raped my mother. Get out!" She became more enraged. "Get out! Get out of my house! You're not my grandfather, you're a *rapist!* If you *ever* come anywhere near Kalley or me again, I'll call the police."

Ralph marched out the door and down the driveway.

Lisa screamed out the door, "And stay away from my father. Don't you ever go to see him again! I will be calling the facility to tell them exactly who you are!"

Lisa slammed her front door, shaking the ornate chandelier in her foyer. She melted to the floor, sobbing like a little girl. Forgiveness would take everything. But beyond that, Lisa knew what her mother would have told her: everything is the true price of love.

CHAPTER 42

Family Reconciliation

LISA WAS IN bed for two days before she mustered up the strength to get herself together. She called her job to get an emergency leave of absence and took the first flight out to Connecticut. First, she stopped to see Keith, who had deteriorated further.

Next, she went straight to St. Raphael's Hospital. Her presence caught the staff by surprise. "Oh! We were expecting Ralph. We got used to seeing him every day. He even sat with her all night when she was critical. We haven't seen him for a few days." Lisa smiled and nodded. "He needed to go home. Would you mind showing me to my sister's room, please?"

Seeing Kalley stopped Lisa's heart for a moment. Her hair was matted and the room had a rank stench in it. She was asleep, and her sheets were soiled.

Furious, Lisa pulled the call cord. "I want to see a doctor for a meeting. Right now."

When two doctors showed up, they motioned for Lisa to follow them outside. Lisa shut the door behind her. The doctors did most of the talking, and Lisa listened deferentially. Kalley had come out of her coma, they told her, but her memory was foggy. She didn't know who she was or how she wound up in the hospital. Her right side was partially paralyzed and she would need unusually extensive rehabilitation with ongoing physical therapy. For the time being, she had the mental capacity of a six-year-old.

Lisa sat down and tried to take deep breaths. She wiped away tiny tears. She couldn't help but remember the promise she'd made to her mother. She remembered it all—how Ralph raped her mother, and yet somehow her mother had still found it in her heart to save his life. Lisa also remembered how she promised her mother that if her father or she weren't around, she would look out for Kalley, in spite of everything her sister had done.

With that thought, Lisa went to the nurses' station.

"Why is my sister dirty? When was she last cleaned up? I'd like to have her cleaned up immediately because I'm taking her out of here today."

The head nurse apologized profusely. "I'm so sorry. We've been under-staffed. When her grandfather was here, he made sure she stayed clean around the clock. But please don't take her out yet. She's not ready to be released."

Lisa raised her voice. "If you say one more word to me, and don't get my sister cleaned up and ready to get out of here, I'll call the newspapers, the police department, and the television stations and tell them about your wretched conditions."

All was silent as the nursing staff scrambled. They bathed Kalley and got her ready to go. They wheeled her out and into the garage, where Lisa and the staff transferred Kalley into the rental car. From there, Lisa drove six hours straight until she got back to her home in DC.

The next day she called her section chief and requested a family leave extension; however, it was denied. She took the day off to get Kalley settled in.

->=◉ ◉=<-

Lisa did whatever caring for Kalley required. It was much harder than she expected, and without any family in the area, she spent a lot of time at home.

The NSA section chief gave Lisa a parachute package, but was very clear: he would not recommend her to other government agencies if they called.

The man she had been dating for a few months stopped calling her. Lisa figured he had moved on because she didn't have much time for him.

Without a long-term plan for the house, and with no reason to live in the same expensive neighborhood, she sold her house and rented a small, cramped one–bedroom apartment near George Washington University Hospital.

Lisa slept on the sofa so Kalley could be more comfortable in the bedroom. It was a difficult situation because the insurance only paid for the visits and the therapy, but not for the transportation. It was a long rough haul, but Lisa held on.

She kept the memory of the promise to her mother in her heart. She knew her mother would not have it any other way. She worked and prayed and took care of Kalley until she was stable enough to start looking for a new job.

She registered Kalley for disability benefits. As the days went by, Lisa began to feel an unfamiliar but transcendent aura of peace pass over her more and more frequently. Eventually, it became normal. Even though life was usually busy and demanding, Lisa smiled more than she had in over a decade.

After about two months, Kalley had eighty percent use of the right side of her body. Lisa made flash cards for at-home therapy and helped Kalley with her speech therapy. Gradually, more of Kalley's memory returned. They both began to remember good times from their childhood. They laughed as they told stories of when they were little girls. "Remember when we fought over the same toy and Mom made us hold hands?" Lisa laughed. Kalley, exerting all her effort, reached out and grasped Lisa's hand. Lisa smiled and blinked hard.

Lisa called Keith often, even though he never remembered their conversations and rambled incessantly. She often talked with Betty, who told her that Richard's body had been found in a nearby park.

One year after Lisa had brought Kalley to D.C., Kalley re-enrolled in college. She transferred her prior credits and chose to major in web design. She set a goal of owning a home-based business after graduating with her Bachelor's. Lisa worked as an IT security consultant for several local businesses, which allowed her to accommodate her schedule to Kalley's needs.

A year later, Li'l Rich was released from Juvenile Camp. Because of his excellent behavior, the judge released him to stay with Kalley and Lisa, who had found a small house in Falls Church. Richie, as he insisted they call him, agreed to go to a nearby high school, and worked part time after school in the evenings. He contributed his check to the household.

One Sunday, Lisa cooked Cornish hens, wild rice, and a large salad. "Just like Mom used to make," Kalley said, smiling, eyes brimming with the memory. Lisa, Kalley and Richie sat around the small table, held hands, bowed their heads. Lisa led the family in prayer. "Thank you, Heavenly Father, for the bond you've restored amongst us. We are blood to each other, but we're saved by the bond of your blood, Lord Jesus, because you gave your life for us. Thank you for Kalley's health and strength. Thank you for Richie's presence and progress. Bless his steps as he goes out and makes his way in the world as a young Black man. Please keep him safe and on the right track. Let us always forgive each other and love each other the way you taught us."

"Amen," Kalley and Richie agreed.

"Let's dig in," Lisa said, beaming with pride and love at her family. She grinned and sighed contentedly as she picked up the salad bowl and extended it toward Kalley. Kalley gripped it securely, then slowly transferred greens and vegetables to her plate. She turned to Richie, who smiled the charming smile Kalley had once seen his father give her all the time. Kalley handed him the bowl, and he put the bowl down on top of his plate. "Thanks, Ma! I'll be done with this in a minute," he quipped, reaching for the dressing. Lisa and Kalley laughed as Richie moved the bowl off his plate and scooped out a large helping of salad before handing the bowl back to Lisa.

Acknowledgements

MY CHILDREN, ALEXIS and Alexzae Tyson, Quandre Duarte for being the ultimate reason that I strive and make progress in this life.

My uncle, Sir Ronnie Tyson for the all of his support, encouragement and direction. You have always believed in my vision.

Samuel Moore and Sebiena Davis, my ultimate support team.

Andrew MacPhail and Joanne De Simone for your creative input and invaluable guidance.

Ted Maynard of (**M.A.C**) Media Arts Center.

Michael Foster of Foster Co LLC.

Why I wrote this book

EVERYTHING I WRITE was born and inspired in January 1991 on my 24th birthday. I saw the film *"Straight Out Of Brooklyn"* and it gave me hope, awakening the knowledge that in spite of race, upbringing and personal struggles one thing holds true; the freedom of expression. I wanted to share my experiences with the world through three of the most powerful sources (outside of music) theater, books and film.

About the author

Alex Tyson was born in Wilson, N.C. and currently lives in New Haven, CT. He is a published author of the novel *"Family Affair"* which has been revised and re-released as *"A Compton Chick"*, under Urban Books based in NYC. Alex wanted to reach a much broader audience and increase the momentum of his writing career as an author to complement his newly found passion as a producer. With the development of his production company FamilyMan Entertainment, he is both excited and blessed for his ability to share future projects with his community and the world alike. Aspiring to break into the film industry.

(Please go to the website and leave your comments and questions about Blood Bond and your contact information for upcoming events).

Website: familyman-ent.com
Email: familymanent@hotmail.com
Phone: (203)-627-9444
Facebook: Alex Tyson Familyman
Book Price: $19.95